# GUESS WHO'S COOKING DINNER

# GUESS WHO'S COOKING DINNER

## Maria Adams Bell

WALKER AND COMPANY
NEW YORK

**Photo Credits**

Marion Anderson—courtesy of Hurok Attractions; Mike Arrabia—Fabian Bachrach; Josephine Baker—Studio Armand, LaHabana, Cuba; Christiaan Barnard—Courtesy of Department of Cardiac Surgery, The University of Cape Town; Shirley Bassey—courtesy of United Artists Records; Maria Adams Bell—Paul Duckworth, photography; Debby Boone—courtesy of International Creative Management; George Burns and Gracie Allen—from the collection of the Memory Shop, NYC; Cantinflas—courtesy of Columbia Pictures, Posa Films Internacional, S.A.; Carter family—official photograph: The White House, Washington D.C.; Mrs. Clark Clifford—Brooks, Bethesda, Md.; Sammy Davis, Jr.—Maurice Seymour, Puerto Rico; John Denver—courtesy RCA Records and Tapes; Duke Ellington—James J. Kriegsmann, NY; Totie Fields—courtesy of Howard Hinderstein, management; Peggy Fleming—Fred Westheimer, William Morris Agency, Beverly Hills, Ca.; Gerald Ford—official photograph: The White House, Washington D.C.; Henry Ford II—courtesy of Ford Motor Co.; Joe Franklin—courtesy of WOR-AM; Judy Garland—courtesy of Metro Goldwyn Mayer; Irving Goldman—Editta Sherman, NYC; Mrs. Barry Goldwater—Arizona Photographic Associates Incorporated; Lord Arthur Goodhart—Conway Studios; John F. Kennedy—© Fabian Bachrach; Moon Landrieu—© Karsh, Ottawa; Robert O. Lowery—official photograph: New York Fire Department; Barry Manilow—photo: Lee Gurst; Johnny Mathis—courtesy of Mahoney/Wasserman; Julia Meade—Charles Caron, NYC; Jack Mitchell—Jack Mitchell, NYC; Agnes Nixon—James J. Kriegsmann, NY; Marion Preminger—M. Blechman; Mrs. Yitzhak Rabin—Chase, Washington; Jean-Pierre Rampal—courtesy of Colbert Artists Management Inc.; A. Philip Randolph—Conway Studios; Charles Rangel—Peter G. Urba, Amsterdam, NY; Martha Raye—NBC photo; Rex Reed—Blume; Willis Reed—courtesy of the New York Knicks; Debbie Reynolds—courtesy of Metro Goldwyn Mayer; Nelson Rockefeller—Halsman, NY; Anwar el-Sadat—courtesy of the Embassy of The Arab Republic of Egypt, Washington D.C.; Beverly Sills—Christian Steiner; Syd Simons—Maurice Seymour, Chicago; Carl Stokes—Geddes; Donna Summer—courtesy of Casablanca Record and Film Works; Sophie Tucker—Maurice Seymour, NY; Liv Ullman—C. Brownie Harris, NYC; Cyrus Vance—Department of State photograph

First published in the United States of America in 1979 by the Walker Publishing Company, Inc.

Published simultaneously in Canada by Beaverbooks, Limited, Pickering, Ontario

Trade ISBN: 0-8027-0614-2
Paper ISBN: 0-8027-7141-6

Library of Congress Catalog Card Number: 78-58621

Printed in the United States of America

10 9 8 7 6 5 4 3 2 1

# Contents

*I lovingly dedicate this book to the source of its inspiration:*
*you wonderful people from all over the world who made it possible*
*and*
*to the memory of two wonderful ladies—*
*The Honorable Dr. Marion Mill Preminger*
*(Mrs. Albert Mayer)*
*and*
*Miss Sophie Tucker.*

The Hon. Dr. Marion Mill Preminger
Consulat Genéral de la République Gabonaise

Miss Sophie Tucker

# Foreword

*We all know stars can eat, but can they cook?* Maria Adams Bell's Guess Who's Cooking Dinner *has to be the best answer anyone has come up with yet. I know one recipe that's quick and surefire. And if you don't like "Chiles Rellenos," there are some 159 other dishes to choose from. With this cast and this menu how can any party not be a hit? Sure, the next best thing to dining with Robert Redford may not be eating his bread, but you'll at least be sure to get your fill.*

*I am especially pleased to be introducing Maria's cookbook since I know it has been a longtime dream of hers. When as a child I sat backstage in the dressing room while my mother performed, Maria occasionally baby-sat for me. Considering what a little terror I was, I know her job wasn't easy. No one could keep me out of the hats, dresses and makeup. Maria was always gentle and understanding, and I know my whole family felt a special warmth for her.*

*For this great collection of star-studded recipes, for the thousands of exciting meals I'm sure these dishes will become and for the good cause to which the proceeds from this book will go—the construction of a twenty-four-hour child-care center for the children of working families and for senior citizens—here's a long-deserved rave: Bravo!*

LIZA MINNELLI

# Introduction

When it comes to food, even the greatest stars become just plain folks. For thirty years I was private secretary, hostess and gourmet specialist in the homes of three celebrated personalities, and I have often been amazed at how many guests had an extensive knowledge of gourmet cooking. Of course, this really shouldn't be all that surprising. For anyone in the entertainment profession, a trim figure, fresh complexion and boundless energy are a must. Knowing what to eat and how to cook it can be as important as raw talent—and how hungry these "stars" often were for new recipes! For twenty-two years I was privileged to work for Miss Sophie Tucker, and I remember how, many times, I would be discussing the dinner menu with her while she sat with friends, and one of her guests—it was often Joan Crawford or some such star—would jump up and say, "Maria, let's make it together!" And we would! Jerry Lewis you couldn't keep out of Miss Tucker's pantry, and when I was working for Arline Judge, Bing Crosby's smiling face would often pop into the kitchen and beg for a taste of "whatever smelled so delicious."

People are often surprised to hear that the parties of Hollywood folks were, in my experience, always delightfully informal. Any formality was reserved for the arrangement of the flowers, the table setting and the preparation of the food. The guests were so friendly that it could often be disarming—a fact I learned my very first day in Hollywood—and therein lies a tale.

Imagine a young girl of twenty who had never been outside of her home town of New Orleans suddenly up and running all the way to Hollywood. Like many young women in the thirties, I grew up reading the movie magazines. The contrasts between life with my family and the gay life of the stars made my head spin. My father died when I was a baby and, though I was fortunate enough to have a unique mother, my brothers and sisters and I all worked from a young age to make ends meet—I cooked my first complete Creole meal for the entire family when I was seven. But in the summer of 1933 I had just graduated from Xavier University with a business degree, and I knew the opportunities for blacks in the South were limited. I had seen the jobs my mother had had to take, and I was determined that my life would be different. I just knew something was waiting for me in that magical land I read so much about. So I bought a one-way ticket for Los Angeles and three days later I arrived: a perky, fresh-faced woman just out of her teens with a thick Southern drawl and five dollars to her name.

I headed straight for the studio lot and met my first star before I even got there. A few blocks shy of the studios a handsome Cadillac was parked in the shade, and in the back seat reading his fan mail sat Clark Gable. I knew if I was going to make it I was going to have to push, so I poked my head through the window, gave him my sweetest Southern smile and told him I was looking for the studios. To my delight he gave me a big smile back.

"Well, you're headed in the right direction," he said. "Where you from?"

"New Or-leuns. I'm here to find work and meet movie people."

That gave him a big laugh. "And you think you're going to walk right in and do just that? Don't you know those guards don't let just anyone in?'' He looked at me a long time, shook his head and smiled again. "Here, I'll write you a note," he said, and he gave me one that said, "Please admit Maria Adams. She'll be no trouble to anyone." That note was not entirely prophetic—I was twenty, after all—but it did begin a long and cherished friendship with Clark Gable and it did work on the guards.

Not two minutes after I was inside the gates I met my future employer. She practically ran me over with her scooter bike. "Hey, want a ride?" Arline Judge asked me.

"No," I said, "I'm looking for work."

"Well, then, come to lunch. I want to talk to you."

"What about my job?"

"That's what I want to talk to you about."

And so it was that on my first day in Hollywood I sat down to steak and french fries and girl talk at the MGM commissary with Arline Judge and Judy Garland.

They were gay times and Arline threw wonderful parties. Then married to director Wesley Ruggles, Arline was also in her early twenties and one of the rising young starlets at Twentieth-Century Fox. Parties at the Ruggles featured all the big names: Clark Gable and Carole Lombard, Bing Crosby and his wife, Dixie Dunbar, Jean Harlow and many others.

Actually even more important to me at the time were Frank and Irma, Arline's French chef and his wife. From my childhood I knew the mainstays of Creole cooking—gumbo soups, swordfish supreme, lobster thermidor and the distinctive Creole sauces—but Frank and Irma taught me the basics of Cordon Bleu gourmet cooking and a broader range of dishes. Most of Arline's guests liked seafood—we often had salmon mousse or crème bouillabaisse or, for a change of taste, game terrine, galantines—but her parties were famous for her desserts: exotic soufflés, crêpes Suzette, *Kirschtorten* or *pots de crème*. These delicacies brought Bing Crosby and many others back again and again for more than a taste.

In 1937 Arline threw over her husband and her career to marry Dan Topping, then owner of the Brooklyn Dodgers football team. She moved East. I stayed behind. Through the grapevine Mr. Song-and-Dance Man himself, Harry Richman, heard that I was free and soon hired me to act as hostess and private secretary, to prepare the menu and supervise the cooking. An immaculate dinner jacket, top hat and evening stick were the Richman trademarks as much as his popular songs about high living: "Puttin' on the Ritz," "On the Sunny Side of the Street," "Birth of the Blues," and many others. When Harry Richman did something, he did it in a big way. He was famous for giving away $10 gold pieces when he rode down Broadway in his Rolls Royce. His twenty-six-room showplace, "Ritzland," on Biscayne Island off Miami Beach was *the* gathering place for the stars, and they came in flocks: Jean Harlow, Clara Bow (once his fiancée), Hedy Lamarr, Fats Waller, Joan Bennett, Jack Dempsey, Tony Martin, Martha Raye and many more. At Ritzland I ran the parties, and Harry gave parties of all types: house parties, plane parties (Harry had been the twenty-ninth person to fly the Atlantic in a monoplane the year before) and yacht parties. All of them required a spectacular spread of food. Harry would typically shanghai ten of his friends aboard his yacht early in the morning and sail, eat and drink until late that night. Every lunch featured an aspic mold filled with seafood. Dinner would usually be Southern fried chicken, spinach soufflé and duchess potatoes. One of the greatest yacht parties occurred by chance. Harry invited Louis Armstrong and some of his friends aboard one time, and they took over the bandstand and jammed all night.

I remember one guest in particular at one of Harry's parties in 1941. She told me I reminded her of a girl who once worked for her, and she told Harry, "I'm going to get that girl one day." She did. Not much later I was working for Harry during the day and helping Miss Sophie Tucker backstage when she played The Beachcombers in Miami. By the end of the year I had not only begun working for her full time, I was enrolled in the Cordon Bleu Cooking School in Paris, a long-desired goal.

Of course, everyone knows Sophie Tucker as the original "Red Hot Mamma," but, actually, except for the parties she gave, Miss Tucker led a very quiet life. Her favorite evenings were quiet dinners on a tray for two: stuffed pocket of veal, meat loaf or a mixed salad with oil and vinegar and a fruit dessert. This would be followed by a game of gin rummy with close friends Peggy Bramson and Eve Block.

Miss Tucker could just as easily be called "the original Yiddish Mamma." Any hungry actor who needed a meal knew he could find one at 737 Park Avenue. She loved to give young talent a break and, in fact, was responsible for introducing promising youngsters to each other at the Five O'Clock Club in Atlantic City. Dean Martin and Jerry Lewis made frequent return engagements at her parties.

When she threw a party, Sophie Tucker spared no pains. Her favorite dish was flaming beef with onion pie; gefilte fish and seafood supreme were close runners-up. She always insisted on featuring either a mimosa salad or mixed greens, served with Camembert, Edam or blue cheese. I introduced one dish that Miss Tucker loved. I called it "Medley of Vegetables," and the butler would bring it around from person to person during the meal. In the center would be a cauliflower cooked in milk, surrounded by beets cut in the shape of flowers, baby carrots, tiny green beans and several other vegetables, all served with hollandaise sauce. This offered not only a variety of choices but an eye-catching arrangement of color, as well. For dessert the favorite of the house was Bavarian cream with fresh fruit.

On some occasions Miss Tucker would indulge the favorite tastes of her guests. For George Burns and Gracie Allen, for instance, it would be stuffed cabbage or brisket of beef with potato pancakes and applesauce. For Jerry Lewis, fricassee of chicken. I kept a file of the guests' favorite dishes. In fact, the recipes in this book for Duke Ellington, Sammy Davis Jr. and Jack Benny (and Mary Livingston) are from this very file. The range of guests at her parties was extraordinary. Besides those mentioned above they included Milton Berle, Mr. and Mrs. Ted Lewis, Earl Mountbatten, Mr. and Mrs. Lew Walters (parents of Barbara Walters), Earl Wilson, Ed Sullivan, Abe Lastfogel (president of William Morris Agency), Joe E. Lewis and many others, along with, of course, Miss Tucker's ever-present brother, Moses Abuza, whom you were sure to find at the buffet table.

Many of the recipes in this book grew out of my own personal relationship with the person named, and a few of these merit a special mention.

Anyone familiar with the career of Judy Garland knows she had a most difficult life. During a particularly agonizing period of her last years, she asked me to help her backstage. This turned out to be one of the most memorable nights of my life. After she had given two trying performances, and even though the audience had left, Miss Garland still refused to go home. She went onstage and for three straight hours she sang her heart out to an audience of one. I thought she never sounded better. During the few quiet moments of that stormy evening we discussed family, food and other areas of common interest. I include the recipe she described to me then as a memento of that unforgettable night.

Marilyn Monroe, who had a similarly tragic life, told me she would dish up her "Vegetable Cocktail" whenever she needed an energy boost. "It's a real pick-me-up," she would say.

Montgomery Clift did not like to eat at all. When he did eat, he didn't like to chew. His cook, an older woman and a close friend of mine, would often call me when he was in one of his deep depressions. "I can't get him to eat a thing," she would say, "but maybe if you would make him something, something soft, and bring it, maybe he would eat it." So I would make some chicken soup or beef tea and coax him into eating it. His favorite dish was gazpacho and that's what I've included here.

Other recipes come from the voluminous correspondence I have conducted over the past twelve years, correspondence I have pursued for a cause. It has long been my dream to create a twenty-four-hour children's center in New York City. It was to fulfill this dream that The Educational Guild for Tots to Seniors Foundation Inc. was formed, and all royalties derived from the sale of this book have been donated to it. The proposed center will provide continuous social services for children of working parents plus live-in facilities for a limited number of senior citizens who will become actively involved in the center's programs.

I had originally intended to write my own cookbook to achieve my child-care center dream. Then, in 1962, as I was standing on the Judean Hills of Israel, I saw all around me what could be achieved through the concerted effort of a people with a dream and the will to realize it. I saw then how much better it would be to create a cookbook of the treasured recipes of celebrated people—those I knew personally and others I could contact. I have since campaigned (by letter, in person or by phone) for the favorite recipes, photographs and authorizations featured in this cookbook. It brings me special pleasure to include here the recipes not only of the personalities of today, but also those who have passed on. I hope these favorite dishes will go some small way toward immortalizing the joy and happiness they gave to so many. Each recipe has been kitchen-tested to Cordon Bleu standards so I can safely say: they're all superb!

This book could not be a reality if it were not for the encouragement, expertise and inspiration of the following individuals: Messrs. M.C. and Charles Abuza; Miss Cindy Adams; Mr. and Mrs. Frank Altschul; Drs. Judith and John Antrobus; my dear husband, Thomas E. Bell; Mrs. Sam (Peggy) Bramson; Joseph Brill, Esq.; Mr. Lewis Chambers; Mr. Steven Crocker; The Hon. Irving Goldman; Mrs. Irving Held; The Hon. Louis J. Lefkowitz; Vivienne W. Nearing, Esq.; Dr. Robert H. Schuller; Mr. Richard Slate; Mr. W. Clement Stone; Mrs. Susan Wagner; Mr. Wilson W. Woodbeck; Mr. and Mrs. Isidore Newman II; and my publishers, Mr. and Mrs. Samuel S. Walker, Jr.

To my editor Miss Inez M. Krech I express deep gratitude for her superb professionalism.

Only with hearts, minds and hands joined in a continued effort will we eventually merit not only God's blessings but the gratitude of generations of lost children to whose welfare and benefit our cause is totally dedicated.

MARIA ADAMS BELL

# 1

## APPETIZERS
## AND
## FIRST COURSES

# ROBERT MERRILL

# Chicken Livers Chasseur

6 baked patty shells
1 pound fresh chicken livers
3 tablespoons flour
2 ounces unsalted butter
¼ cup chopped onion
½ cup chopped mushrooms
1¼ cups hot water
¼ tablespoon soy sauce
½ teaspoon salt
¼ teaspoon black pepper

Rinse livers, trim if necessary, and chop. Toss with flour until all pieces are coated. Melt butter in a skillet and sauté onion and mushrooms until onion is translucent. Add liver pieces and cook and stir until livers are browned. Add hot water, soy sauce, salt and pepper. Simmer for 8 minutes. Spoon into patty shells and serve hot. Makes 6 servings.

# SUSAN WAGNER

# Cheese Straws

¼ pound unsalted butter (1 stick)
2 cups grated Cheddar cheese
1½ cups sifted flour
½ tablespoon baking powder
½ tablespoon salt
½ teaspoon red pepper

Preheat oven to 350°F. Cream the butter. Add grated cheese and cream well together. Sift remaining ingredients together and mix into butter and cheese. Roll out on a lightly floured board to a sheet ⅛ inch thick. Cut into strips ½ inch wide and 6 inches long. Place on an ungreased, unfloured baking sheet, and bake for about 15 minutes, until delicately browned. Do not overbake them. Makes about 3 dozen.

2

# BILL "BOJANGLES" ROBINSON

# Cocktail Meatballs

6 large onions
3 small onions
2 garlic cloves
3 tablespoons melted chicken fat
    (more as needed)
2 teaspoons salt
¼ teaspoon black pepper
1 teaspoon crumbled dried orégano
1 teaspoon paprika
3 slices of white bread
3 pounds beef chuck, ground
¼ teaspoon monosodium glutamate
1½ cups ketchup

Cut large onions into very thin slices. Chop small onions fine and set aside. Peel and mince garlic and add half of it to chopped onions. Melt chicken fat in a large deep skillet, and sauté sliced onions and half of garlic until golden brown. Season with a little of the salt, pepper and orégano, and sprinkle with paprika. Keep stirring onions so they do not burn. Remove crusts from bread and tear slices to bits. Soak bread in cold water to cover while onions are cooking. Put ground chuck in a large bowl and add soaked bread (do not squeeze out the water). Add chopped onion and garlic mixture to meat, remaining seasoning and orégano, and the monosodium glutamate. Add also half of the sautéed onion slices to the meat. Mix together until bread disappears in the meat; the texture should be light but easy to handle. (More seasoning and herbs can be added if you like.) Shape meat mixture into balls the size of walnuts, and add them to the skillet which still contains the balance of the sliced onions. Cover skillet tightly and simmer the meatballs for about 30 minutes. Uncover and spoon the ketchup over the top; it should cover the meatballs completely. With a metal spoon, gently separate meatballs, as they stick together, and turn them over. Try to distribute the onion slices evenly among meatballs. Again cover pot tightly and simmer for 1½ hours longer. Transfer to a chafing dish, so meatballs can be kept warm, and serve with fondue forks or skewers. Makes about 3 dozen.

## GRACIE ALLEN AND GEORGE BURNS

# Egg Mousse with Seafood Salad

12 eggs, hard cooked
1 cup mayonnaise
1 cup milk

1¼ tablespoons unflavored gelatin
salt and pepper
2 cups shrimp or crab salad

Peel and chop eggs and put in a blender container with mayonnaise. Pour half of the milk into a small bowl and sprinkle gelatin on top. Heat remaining milk in a saucepan. When gelatin is softened, spoon it into hot milk and stir over low heat until dissolved. Add to eggs and blend well. Season with salt and pepper to taste. Spoon into an oiled 4-cup ring mold and chill in refrigerator until set.

At serving time, turn mousse out onto a platter and fill center with shrimp or crab salad. Garnish. Makes 8 servings.

## JOE FRANKLIN

# Broiled Mushrooms with Pâté de Foie Gras

18 large mushrooms
3 tablespoons melted butter
½ teaspoon salt
½ teaspoon black pepper

6 tablespoons pâté de foie gras
½ cup buttered bread crumbs
8 slices of toast, buttered

Wash mushrooms and pat dry; remove stems (use them for another recipe). Brush mushroom caps with melted butter and sprinkle them with salt and pepper. Spoon 1 teaspoon of the pâté into each cap, and sprinkle with about 1¼ teaspoons of the crumbs. Arrange in a buttered shallow baking pan and slide under a preheated broiler about 4 inches from the source of heat. Broil for about 8 minutes, until crumbs are golden brown. Serve 3 mushrooms on a slice of toast. Makes 8 servings.

# DUKE ELLINGTON

# Shrimps in Spicy Sauce

1½ pounds shrimps in shells
¾ cup mayonnaise
¼ cup minced sweet pickles
2 tablespoons minced parsley
1 tablespoon minced capers
2 teaspoons minced scallions (green onions)
2 bunches of watercress

Wash shrimps well in cold water. Place shrimps, without draining, in a saucepan, cover tightly, and steam over low heat for 15 minutes, or until shells turn pink. Drain shrimps, peel them, and remove veins. Mix mayonnaise with pickles, parsley, capers and scallions. Gently fold in shrimps, and chill. Wash watercress, roll in a towel to dry, and discard stems. Arrange sprigs on a low compote, or on individual dishes, and place shrimps and sauce on top. Makes 6 servings.

## PRINCESS GRACE
## OF MONACO

# Pissaladière

*"This is a very old Monégasque specialty and, therefore, one of the favorite dishes in the principality. It is often made at home in Monaco, or one can buy it in any bakery or in the marketplace. Pissaladière is baked all year long and may be eaten hot or cold."*

¾ cup warm water (105° to 115°F.)
olive oil
1 package active dry yeast
2 cups sifted all-purpose flour
salt
2 pounds onions
1 garlic clove

6 large ripe tomatoes
1 cup freshly grated Parmesan cheese
freshly ground black pepper
½ teaspoon crumbled dried rosemary
3 cans (2 ounces each) flat anchovy
    fillets, drained
1 cup (or more) pitted French
    black olives

Pour the water into a small bowl, add 1½ tablespoons olive oil, and sprinkle yeast on top. Stir yeast to dissolve it. Place flour and a pinch of salt in a large bowl, and stir in yeast mixture to form a medium soft dough. Turn out dough onto a lightly floured board and knead for about 10 minutes, until dough is smooth and satiny. Place dough in an oiled bowl, turn over to oil entire surface, and cover with a towel. Let dough rise in a warm place (80° to 85°F.) until doubled in bulk, about 1 hour.

Pour 2 tablespoons olive oil into a large skillet. Peel onions and chop fine. Peel garlic and push through a press into the oil. Add chopped onions, cover, and cook over low heat for 35 minutes, until onions are golden but not browned. Set aside. Peel and quarter tomatoes; press out as many seeds as possible, and chop tomatoes. Place them in a heavy pan and cook uncovered over low heat, stirring occasionally, for 30 minutes, until they are reduced to a thick purée.

Preheat oven to 400°F. Punch down the dough, then place on a lightly floured board and let it rest, covered with a towel, for 5 minutes. Roll out dough to a circle 16 inches in diameter and lift onto a 16-inch pan. Sprinkle dough with the grated cheese. Season onions with a little salt and pepper to taste, then spoon them over the cheese-topped pastry. Season tomato purée with rosemary, then spoon over the onion layer. Separate anchovy fillets and crisscross the pie with them. Place an olive in each space, and brush olives with a little olive oil. Bake in a preheated oven until crust is browned and filling bubbly and hot, 20 to 30 minutes. Cut into slices and serve very hot. Makes 8 to 12 servings.

6

# THE HONORABLE MOON LANDRIEU

# Stuffed Artichokes

5 large artichokes
1 lemon, halved
¾ pound saltines, crushed
½ cup Italian bread crumbs with cheese
5 garlic cloves, peeled and slivered
4 ounces Parmesan cheese, grated
1 cup chopped fresh parsley,
    or ½ cup dried parsley flakes
salt
1 cup olive oil, or more

Wash artichokes well; cut off stems to make a level base, and rub base with a lemon half. With scissors snip off the pointed tips of the leaves, and rub lemon pieces over all cut edges. Set artichokes upside down to drain.

Mix well the crushed saltines, bread crumbs, garlic, cheese and parsley. Scoop the crumb mixture into the artichokes, separating the leaves to press stuffing between leaves and in the center. Set the artichokes in a pot that holds them snugly, and pour salted water (1 teaspoon to 1 quart) around them, about halfway up the artichokes. Pour olive oil lavishly over each one. Cover the pot, bring water to a boil, and boil artichokes for 1 hour, until tender. Test by pulling off a leaf and tasting it. It may be necessary to add more boiling water during cooking; the pan should not become dry. Makes 5 servings.

# MARY MARTIN

# Aspic

3 calf's feet
1 pound slices of veal shin
1 onion, peeled and sliced
1 carrot, scraped and sliced
1 celery rib
4 parsley sprigs
1 garlic clove, peeled
3 peppercorns, crushed
1 teaspoon salt
2 egg whites, well beaten
1 can (10 ½ ounces) clear beef consommé
4 cups tomato juice or water

Have butcher clean calf's feet well, and chop the slices of veal shin. Put in a large heavy pot and add vegetables, garlic, peppercorns and salt. Cover with at least 3 quarts of water. Bring to a boil, then reduce to a simmer. Skim the surface often for the first hour. Cook for 2½ to 3 hours, or until the calf's feet boil to pieces. Strain the broth and let it cool. Remove every bit of fat from the surface.

Return broth to the kettle and stir in the egg whites. Slowly bring to a boil, stirring, then set the heat so aspic barely simmers and let it cook undisturbed until egg whites have coagulated on the top, 30 to 45 minutes. With a skimmer lift off the egg mass, then strain aspic into a clean pot. Add the clear consommé and the 4 cups water. Season if necessary. Makes 6 to 8 cups.

To use aspic, pour into a large mold and refrigerate until firm. Or spoon over small amounts of pâté in tiny molds for first-course serving. Or pour over pâté in a large ring mold. Cubes of aspic are delicious served with hearts of lettuce, with French dressing. Aspic made with tomato juice and molded in a ring can be filled with any seafood or seafood salad.

# SOPHIE TUCKER

# Gefilte Fish

1 ½ pounds whitefish
1 ½ pounds pike
salt
3 medium-size onions, peeled
2 medium-size carrots, scraped
1 parsley sprig
1 celery root with leaves
4⅓ cups cold water
3 eggs
1 tablespoon cracker meal
1 teaspoon sugar
¼ teaspoon black pepper

Start this the night before for best results. Wash, dress and fillet whitefish and pike. Reserve heads, skin and all large bones, wrap and refrigerate. Salt the fillets and refrigerate overnight.

Use a 4-quart pot. Cut 2 onions into thin slices and carrots into round slices. Cut parsley and celery root and leaves into small pieces. Drop all these into the pot with 4 cups of the water. Add the reserved fish heads, skin and bones, bring liquid to a boil, and simmer for 10 minutes.

While the fish broth cooks, chop the salted fillets and remaining onion. Add remaining ⅓ cup water, a little at a time, as you chop. Add eggs, cracker meal, 1 teaspoon salt, the sugar and ⅛ teaspoon pepper. Chop all together; the mixture should feel sticky against the chopper. Form into patties, and place them carefully in the fish broth on top of bones and vegetables; the liquid should just cover patties. Simmer for 1 hour.

Taste broth; add remaining pepper and more salt if necessary. Cover pot and simmer for 2 hours longer, shaking the pot once in a while. Uncover pot and simmer for 30 minutes longer. Remove fish patties to a serving bowl, and cool. Strain the cooking liquid, and cool. Chill both patties and liquid in refrigerator; liquid will jell. (Cooking liquid and gefilte fish can be jellied in a fish mold that holds about 8 cups.) Makes 12 servings.

9

# BARBARA CARTLAND

# Smoked Salmon Pâté

*"This is a fabulous dish and I have never known a man who was not thrilled with it and relaxed and very amenable after eating it. Every ingredient is good for health and sex,"* says Barbara Cartland.

2 ounces smoked salmon
3 ounces pot cheese or cottage cheese
½ cup cream
1 teaspoon snipped fresh chives
1 teaspoon fresh lemon juice
salt and pepper

Pound the salmon in a mortar. Add cheese and continue pounding until mixture is smooth. Mix in cream, chives, lemon juice, and salt and pepper to taste. Serve with hot toast and butter. Makes about 1 cup.

# MARILYN MONROE

# Vegetable Cocktail

4 small carrots
2 ripe tomatoes
2 celery ribs
½ pound fresh mushrooms
¼ pound fresh green beans
½ pound fresh spinach
½ pound fresh green peas
juice of 1 lemon
½ teaspoon Worcestershire sauce
¼ teaspoon salt
¼ teaspoon black pepper
2 dashes of Tabasco
2 ice cubes

Scrape and trim carrots; peel and trim tomatoes; wash and trim celery, mushrooms, green beans and spinach. Shell green peas. Slice carrots, tomatoes and celery. Drop vegetables into the container of an electric blender, and add lemon juice and seasonings. Cover container and whirl at medium speed for 6 seconds. While motor is running, remove center cover and drop in ice cubes. Makes 8 servings.

# 2

## SOUPS

# THE HONORABLE BASIL A. PATERSON

# Black Bean Soup

4 cups dried black beans
1 small beef shin, cut into
    crosswise slices
2 celery ribs, minced
1 onion, minced
2 beef bouillon cubes
2 bay leaves
1 tablespoon Worcestershire sauce
1 tablespoon Beau Monde seasoning
few allspice berries
few whole cloves
1 teaspoon salt
pepper

2 tablespoons dry sherry wine
1 hard-cooked egg, chopped
juice of 1 lemon, strained
snipped fresh chives

Soak beans in water overnight. Next morning, transfer beans to a large heavy pot, add beef shin, and cover with fresh cold water. Bring to a boil, then simmer until the meat falls from the shin bones. Discard bones. Transfer beans, part at a time, to a blender container, and purée. (Add a little of the cooking water if necessary to help the action of the blender.)

Put puréed beans in a large pot with 5 cups of the cooking water and add celery, onion, bouillon cubes and all the seasonings, with pepper to taste. Bring again to a boil and simmer for 30 minutes. Add sherry, chopped egg and lemon juice. Sprinkle chives over each bowl of soup. Makes 6 or more servings.

14

## THE HONORABLE
## MURIEL HUMPHREY

# Beef Soup

1½ pounds beef stew meat
1 beef soup bone (from chuck)
1 teaspoon salt
½ teaspoon black pepper
2 bay leaves
1 cup chopped celery
1 cup chopped cabbage
4 medium-size carrots, scraped and sliced
½ cup chopped onion

2 cans (16 ounces each) plum tomatoes
1 tablespoon Worcestershire sauce
1 beef bouillon cube
pinch of dried orégano

Cover meat and soup bone with cold water in a heavy 3-quart kettle. Add salt, pepper and bay leaves. Bring slowly to a boil while preparing vegetables. Reduce soup to a simmer and add celery, cabbage, carrots and onion. Simmer for at least 2½ hours, until meat is very tender. Remove bone and bay leaves. Lift out meat and cut into bite-size pieces. Return meat pieces to soup and add remaining ingredients. Simmer for 30 minutes longer. Makes 8 servings.

## GEORGE MEANY

# Vegetable-Beef Soup

3 pounds beef chuck, cubed
3 beef marrowbones, cracked
1 teaspoon salt
3 celery ribs, cut into 1-inch pieces
3 carrots, scraped and cut up
3 onions, peeled and sliced
2 cups canned stewed tomatoes

1 cup canned tomato sauce
½ teaspoon Worcestershire sauce
pinch of dried basil
pinch of dried orégano
¼ cup uncooked herb rice
½ pound medium noodles

Place beef and marrowbones in a large pot and cover with water. Add ½ teaspoon salt. Bring to a boil, cover, and simmer for 2 hours. Add remaining ingredients except noodles and simmer for 25 minutes longer, or until all vegetables and the beef cubes are tender and the rice fully cooked. Taste, and add remaining salt if necessary. Discard bones. While soup cooks, separately cook noodles in lots of boiling water until just done; drain. Serve some noodles in each bowl of soup. Makes 8 or more servings.

# CRAIG CLAIBORNE

# Fish Soup

2 pounds dressed firm-fleshed fish
    (striped bass, sea bass, carp)
2 dozen mussels
2 dozen clams
6 small squids (optional)
¼ cup olive oil
1 large onion, chopped
3 garlic cloves, peeled and minced
3 celery ribs, minced
1 tablespoon whole saffron
2 cups canned peeled plum tomatoes
    with basil
2 cups water
1 cup dry white wine
2 teaspoons minced fresh thyme,
    or ½ teaspoon dried
1 bay leaf

1 teaspoon fennel seeds, crushed
Tabasco
1 large fresh tomato, peeled and chopped
salt and pepper
¼ cup chopped fresh parsley
1 tablespoon (or more) Pernod, Ricard,
    or other anise-flavored liqueur
8 Croutons (recipe follows)

Rinse fish, pat dry, and cut into large serving pieces. Scrub mussels and remove beards. Scrub clams. Dress squids: discard head and pen, and cut into 2-inch pieces. Heat 2 tablespoons of the oil in a large deep saucepan. Cook onion, garlic, celery and saffron in the oil, stirring occasionally, until most of the moisture has evaporated. Add canned tomatoes, water, wine, thyme, bay leaf, crushed fennel seeds, and Tabasco to taste. Bring to a boil and simmer, uncovered, for 45 minutes. Add pieces of fish, mussels and clams. Cover the saucepan, bring to a boil, and simmer for 20 minutes. Add fresh tomato and squid pieces, and season with salt and pepper to taste. Shake the pan while pouring in remaining oil. Stir in parsley and liqueur. Serve at once in hot soup bowls, with the croutons. Makes 8 servings.

## Croutons

8 slices of crusty day-old bread
    (French or Italian)
1 large garlic clove, split
8 teaspoons olive oil

Preheat oven to 400°F. Rub bread slices on both sides with cut sides of garlic pieces. Brush on both sides with olive oil. Place on a rack or baking sheet and bake, turning once, until golden on both sides.

16

THE HONORABLE
SHIRLEY CHISHOLM

# Royal Melon Broth with Chicken Dumplings

1 winter melon, 10 pounds
1 squab, 1 pound, boned and chopped
¼ pound canned abalone, chopped
½ cup chopped mushrooms
½ cup chopped water chestnuts
½ cup chopped bamboo shoots
2 tablespoons dry sherry wine
2 teaspoons soy sauce
1 tablespoon Beau Monde seasoning
1 teaspoon Bon Appetit seasoning
1 teaspoon salt

1 teaspoon freshly ground pepper
1 teaspoon minced fresh tarragon
1 teaspoon minced fresh parsley
6 cups chicken bouillon, or more
Chicken Dumplings (recipe follows)
2 tablespoons chopped cooked ham
1 cup cooked tiny peas

Wash melon and cut off the top, using a zigzag pattern. Remove all melon seeds. Put next 13 ingredients in the melon and pour in enough chicken bouillon to reach within ½ inch of the top of the melon. Set the melon on a rack over 2 inches of boiling water in a deep kettle. Cover kettle and steam melon over medium heat for 8 hours, adding more boiling water when necessary to keep it at the same level in the kettle. When cooking is finished, lift rack from kettle, and skim fat from the broth. Serve soup with the dumplings, and garnish with ham and peas. Makes 6 servings.

## Chicken Dumplings

4 chicken breasts, boned
3 egg whites
salt and pepper
1 cup fresh heavy cream, approximately

Wash chicken and pat dry. Cut into cubes. Grind in an electric blender, using the unbeaten egg whites as liquid. Season the mixture well with salt and pepper, then force the paste through a sieve into a bowl. Refrigerate paste for 3 hours. Beat in enough of the cream to give the paste a workable texture. Use 2 teaspoons to mold the paste into small balls. Drop them into simmering salted water and cook for 10 minutes. Lift out with a skimmer and drain on paper towels. Serve with hot melon broth. Makes about 3 dozen.

# JIMMY DURANTE

# Chicken Noodle Soup

1 stewing chicken, 5 pounds
2 medium-size carrots, scraped and sliced
1 large celery rib, trimmed and chopped
1 large onion, peeled and sliced
1 tablespoon salt
¼ teaspoon pepper
10 cups water
2 cups fine noodles
chopped fresh parsley

Rinse inside of chicken well with cold water. Place chicken in a 4-quart kettle and add all other ingredients except noodles and parsley. Bring water to a boil, cover the kettle, and simmer for 2 hours, until chicken is tender. Remove chicken from the kettle. When cool enough to handle, discard skin and bones and chill the meat to use another day. Let the broth stand until fat rises to the top, then skim off the fat.

Reheat broth to boiling, then stir in noodles and cook for 10 minutes, until noodles are tender. Ladle soup into heated bowls or soup plates, and sprinkle with chopped parsley. Makes 8 servings.

18

# REX REED

# Shrimp Gumbo

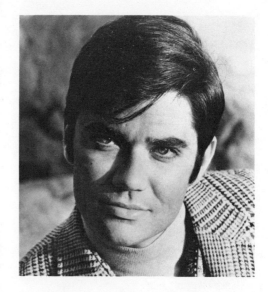

3 tablespoons vegetable oil
3 tablespoons flour
3 cups sliced stemmed fresh okra
2 scallions (green onions),
    white part only, chopped
1 cup chopped onion
1 garlic clove, peeled and minced
1 cup chopped celery
2 heaping tablespoons minced fresh parsley
½ tablespoon salt
freshly ground black pepper
3 tablespoons chopped ham (optional)
2 pounds fresh raw shrimps in shells
2 pounds fresh king crab legs,
    or 1 pound fresh blue crab meat
gumbo filé powder

1 cup chicken stock
2 teaspoons Worcestershire sauce
8 to 10 drops of Tabasco
¼ cup fresh lemon juice
large pinch of dried thyme
2 bay leaves

Use a 4-quart pressure saucepan. Brown oil and flour in it over medium heat, stirring all the while, until the roux is almost black. Add all the vegetables, the salt, and black pepper to taste. Cook, stirring often, until vegetables are slightly softened. Add stock, Worcestershire, Tabasco, lemon juice, herbs and ham, and heat to a simmer.

Peel and devein shrimps. Cut crab legs with a scissors to release meat; discard shells. Or pick over crab meat and discard any bits of cartilage. Add seafood to the saucepan, close cover securely, bring up pressure, and cook for 4 minutes. Cool saucepan at once, remove cover, and stir. Taste, and correct seasoning if needed. Serve at once over fluffy rice flavored with parsley. Sprinkle filé powder over gumbo at the table. Accompany with hot garlic French bread and green salad. Makes 4 to 6 servings.

*Rex Reed's advice:*

*"The pressure saucepan saves time and heat in the summer kitchen, but if you don't have one, the gumbo can be made in a sturdy kettle. In that case, increase chicken stock to 2 quarts, and cook the vegetable and stock mixture for 45 minutes before adding seafood. After adding seafood, cook until shrimps begin to turn pink, no longer. Adjust seasoning to taste; you may need a little more when cooking this way.*

*"Do not add filé powder until cooking is finished, as it becomes stringy when cooked. Without filé, gumbo can be refrigerated or frozen, to be reheated for serving."*

19

PRESIDENT
JOHN F. KENNEDY

# New England Fish Chowder

2 pounds dressed haddock
4½ cups water
2 ounces salt pork, diced
2 onions, peeled and chopped
4 potatoes, peeled and diced
1 cup chopped celery
1 bay leaf, crumbled
1 teaspoon salt

freshly ground black pepper
4 cups milk
2 tablespoons butter

Place haddock in a saucepan with 2 cups of the water. Bring to a boil and simmer for 15 minutes. Pour off and reserve the fish broth. Remove bones from fish. Heat salt pork in a large kettle. Add onions and sauté until golden brown. Add haddock, potatoes, celery, bay leaf, salt, and pepper to taste. Pour in fish broth and remaining 2½ cups water which has been brought to a boil. Simmer the chowder for 45 minutes. Add milk and butter, and simmer for 10 minutes longer. Makes 6 servings.

## MARTHA RAYE

# Garden Bouillon

½ pound green snap beans
1 summer squash
1 small cucumber
1 bunch of watercress
1 turnip
1 carrot
2 small white onions
6 outside lettuce leaves
3 outside celery ribs
3 firm radishes
2 parsley sprigs

2 quarts cold water
½ cup dry sherry wine
vegetable salt

Wash vegetables thoroughly but do not peel them. Trim them as needed, and cut into coarse pieces. Place in a large kettle, cover with the cold water, cover kettle, and simmer for 2 hours. Push everything through a sieve, or through a food mill, or purée in a blender. Return to the kettle, add sherry, and season with vegetable salt to taste. Serve hot in bouillon cups. Makes 8 servings.

## MRS. CLARK CLIFFORD

# Curry Consommé

1 apple
1 Bermuda onion
4 cups prepared consommé
2 cups heavy cream
½ tablespoon curry powder
2 tablespoons snipped fresh chives

Wash apple but do not peel. Remove stem and blossom ends, cut into quarters, and drop into a large saucepan. Peel and quarter onion and add to apple. Pour in consommé and heat to boiling. Cool, then refrigerate overnight. At serving time, strain consommé into a clean saucepan, add cream and curry powder, and heat. Sprinkle 1 teaspoon chives on each serving. Accompany with toasted and buttered split puff crackers. Makes 6 servings.

## JACK MITCHELL

# Cold Yogurt Soup

1 medium-size cucumber
salt
2 cups plain yogurt
2 cups chicken broth
1 tablespoon olive oil
½ garlic clove, peeled
1 tablespoon snipped fresh chives
2 tablespoons minced walnuts
black pepper

Wash and peel cucumber, cut lengthwise into halves, and scoop out seeds. Cut cucumber into small pieces, sprinkle with salt, and let stand for 15 minutes. Rinse and drain. In a large bowl mix yogurt, chicken broth and oil. Put garlic through a press into the mixture and add chives, walnuts, and freshly ground pepper to taste. Fold in cucumber pieces. Refrigerate for 3 hours before serving. Makes 4 to 6 servings.

## MONTGOMERY CLIFT

# Gazpacho

4 medium-size ripe tomatoes
1 large cucumber
1 large onion
2 garlic cloves
1 tablespoon snipped fresh dill
1 teaspoon salt
2 cups chicken broth                    ½ tablespoon ground cuminseed
1 tablespoon lemon juice                ½ large green pepper

Peel and quarter tomatoes, remove as many seeds as possible, and chop. Peel and chop cucumber and onion. Drop the vegetables into a blender container. Peel garlic and push through a press into the vegetables. Add dill and salt and blend until mixture is smooth. Add chicken broth, lemon juice and cuminseed and blend again for about 3 seconds, until very smooth. Refrigerate for several hours. Wash and trim green pepper, discard ribs and seeds, and dice. Spoon gazpacho into chilled bowls, and divide diced pepper among them. Crushed ice may be added if you like. Instead of puréeing the cucumber, it can be diced separately and added to gazpacho with the green pepper. Makes 4 servings.

22

# HELEN HAYES

# Chilled Avocado Soup

2 cups minced leeks
1 cup minced onions
2 ounces butter
1 tablespoon curry powder
3 cups chopped peeled raw potatoes
4 cups chicken broth
2 ripe avocados
2 cups heavy cream
1 teaspoon Tabasco
1 teaspoon salt
½ teaspoon black pepper

Wash leeks well before and after mincing. Cook leeks and onions in the butter in a 2-quart saucepan until onions are wilted. Stir in curry powder, then raw potatoes, and continue to cook over low heat, stirring all the while, for about 8 minutes. Add chicken broth and bring soup to a full boil. Simmer, skimming the surface as necessary, for 30 minutes. Let the soup cool, then purée it, a portion at a time, in an electric blender. Turn the puréed soup into a large mixing bowl.

Peel avocados and remove pits. Dice into the blender container, and add about 1 cup of the puréed soup. Blend until smooth, then mix well with the rest of the soup in the bowl. Stir in cream, Tabasco, salt and pepper. Chill. Serve in chilled glass coupettes or in chilled bouillon cups. Makes 10 servings.

## PEGGY FLEMING JENKINS

# Crème Vichyssoise Glacée

4 leeks
4 medium-size potatoes
4 cups water
2 teaspoons salt
2 cups milk, hot
2 cups light cream, hot

1 cup heavy cream, cold
snipped fresh chives

Wash leeks thoroughly. Discard green part (so soup will be snowy white) and cut white part into fine dice. Peel and dice potatoes. Put vegetables in a 2½-quart saucepan with water and salt and cook slowly for 35 minutes. Push the soup through a sieve, or purée it in a blender. Return purée to the saucepan and add hot milk and hot light cream. Bring almost to a boil and cook for a few minutes to blend the flavors, stirring to prevent scorching. Strain soup through a fine sieve, cool it, stir it, and strain it again. Taste for seasoning; soup should be slightly oversalted to overcome the inhibiting effect of cold on salt. Stir in heavy cream and chill in coldest part of refrigerator. Sprinkle with chives. Makes 8 to 10 servings.

# 3

---

# EGG DISHES, SOUFFLÉS, QUICHES

## JEAN-PIERRE RAMPAL

# Eggs Mamette

6 eggs
2 pounds yellow onions
2 tablespoons oil
1 teaspoon salt
1 teaspoon black pepper
¼ pound unsalted butter
2 tablespoons flour
1½ cups milk, at room temperature
10 ounces Swiss cheese, grated
oil for baking dish

Hard-cook the eggs, crack shells all over, and place in cold water. Peel eggs, then cut them lengthwise into halves; set aside.

Peel and mince onions. Cook them in the oil in a large skillet over low heat, stirring to prevent sticking, until onions are reduced to a purée (this takes some time). Season purée with salt and pepper.

Melt butter in a saucepan, stir in flour, and with a wire whisk bring the mixture to a foam. Slowly whisk in the milk until smooth and blended, then stir in the onion purée. Set aside ½ cup of the grated cheese. With the whisk, mix the rest of the grated cheese into the sauce.

Generously oil a 4-cup baking dish. Spoon some of the onion-cheese sauce in the dish, then add 6 half eggs in a single layer. Add more sauce, then remaining half eggs. If there is sauce left, spoon it over. Sprinkle remaining cheese on top. Place the dish in a preheated 350°F. oven, then at once reduce heat to 300°F. Bake for 20 to 30 minutes, until top is golden. Makes 6 servings.

# MRS. RICHARD NIXON

# Country
# Omelet

1 medium-size potato
1 medium-size yellow onion
2 ounces unsalted butter
16 silver-dollar-size pieces, ⅛ inch thick,
    of cooked hard Virginia ham
8 eggs, beaten
salt and pepper

Peel potato and onion and cut into thin slices. Melt the butter in a 10-inch skillet or omelet pan with heatproof handle. Sauté potato slices until just done; add onion slices and sauté until golden. Add ham pieces and cook until crisp. Add half of the eggs and let them set on the bottom to hold vegetables and ham together. Add remaining eggs and seasoning to taste. Cook, tilting the pan and pushing in the sides of the omelet to let uncooked portion run underneath and cook. Place the skillet under a hot broiler for a minute or two to set the top. Serve warm or cold, cut into wedges. Makes 6 to 8 servings.

## LIZA MINNELLI

# Chiles Rellenos

3 cans (4 ounces each) green chile peppers
1 pound Monterey Jack cheese
1 pound Cheddar cheese
butter for casserole
4 eggs, separated
⅔ cup half and half
1 tablespoon flour
½ teaspoon salt
⅛ teaspoon pepper
2 medium-size tomatoes

Rinse chiles to remove any seeds; chop chiles. Grate both cheeses. Mix cheese and chiles and turn into a well-buttered shallow 2-quart casserole. In a large bowl beat together egg yolks, half and half, flour, salt and pepper, until well blended. With an electric mixer at high speed, or with a rotary beater, beat egg whites until stiff peaks form when beater is withdrawn. Gently fold egg whites into egg-yolk mixture. Pour egg mixture over cheese and chiles and with a fork gently move cheese mixture to let egg batter seep through. Bake in a preheated 325°F. oven for 30 minutes.

Wash and trim tomatoes, and cut them into slices. Arrange slices around the edge of the casserole and bake for 20 minutes longer. Makes 6 to 8 servings.

# TOTIE FIELDS

# Cheese Soufflé

1 tablespoon butter, softened
1 tablespoon grated Swiss cheese
2 tablespoons butter
3 tablespoons flour
¼ teaspoon dry mustard
1 cup milk, hot
½ cup freshly grated Parmesan cheese
½ cup freshly grated Swiss cheese
4 egg yolks
½ teaspoon salt
½ teaspoon white pepper
6 egg whites
½ teaspoon Worcestershire sauce

Use the tablespoon of softened butter to coat the bottom and sides of a 2-quart soufflé dish. Sprinkle the buttered surface with the tablespoon of grated cheese, tipping the dish to spread cheese as evenly as possible on bottom and sides. Set the dish aside.

Preheat oven to 400°F. Melt 2 tablespoons butter in a large saucepan. Stir in flour and mustard, gradually blend in milk, and cook sauce until it is smooth and thick. Add all the cheese. Beat egg yolks lightly and add to the sauce, along with salt and pepper. Cook only until cheese is melted. Set sauce aside to cool.

With a large whisk beat the egg whites until they are so stiff they form small points that stand up without wavering when whisk is withdrawn. Add Worcestershire to the cheese sauce. Stir a spoonful of the beaten egg white into cheese sauce to lighten it. With a spatula lightly fold in the rest of the egg whites, using an over-under cutting motion rather than stirring. Gently spoon the mixture into the prepared dish. For a decorative effect, make a "cap" or "high hat": with a spatula cut a trench about 1 inch deep around the top of the soufflé. Carefully set the dish on the middle shelf of the preheated oven. Immediately reduce oven heat to 375°F. Bake the soufflé for 30 minutes, until it puffs up about 2 inches above the rim of the dish. Serve at once. Makes 6 servings.

# AGNES NIXON

# Mushroom Soufflé

2 pounds fresh mushrooms
4½ ounces butter
4 tablespoons flour
1 cup light cream
3 eggs, separated
salt and pepper
butter for baking dish

Wash mushrooms and roll in a towel to dry. Remove stems; use them for another recipe. Chop caps. Melt 2½ ounces of the butter in a large skillet and sauté chopped mushrooms for 3 to 5 minutes. They will shrink as they cook, and release juices; you will have 2¼ to 2½ cups mushrooms and 1 cup juice, both of which you will use for the soufflé.

In a pan with rounded sides, melt remaining 2 ounces butter. When it bubbles and foams, stir in the flour; cook and stir until thickened. Add the cream and the reserved mushroom juice. Stir and cook over low heat until sauce is thick and smooth. Cool 1 cup of the sauce; the balance, also about 1 cup, can be reserved for a delicious mushroom soup. Mix the cooled cup of sauce with the sautéed mushrooms.

Preheat oven to 350°F. Beat egg yolks until light, then stir them into mushroom mixture. Season well with salt and pepper. (Remember that adding egg whites always reduces flavor.) Beat egg whites until stiff and gently fold into mushroom mixture. Spoon into a buttered 8-cup soufflé dish or casserole. Set the casserole in a shallow pan one fourth full of water. Bake the soufflé for 40 to 50 minutes, or until set. Makes 8 servings.

MRS. JAYMIE B. WILLIAMS

# Spinach Soufflé

2 pounds fresh spinach
2 tablespoons butter
2 tablespoons flour
½ cup milk
½ cup vegetable broth
1 tablespoon lemon juice
¾ teaspoon salt
¼ teaspoon freshly ground black pepper
¼ teaspoon grated nutmeg
4 eggs, separated
butter for baking dish

Wash spinach thoroughly, and drain. Bring ½ cup water to a boil in a large saucepan, add spinach, and cook for 5 minutes. Drain spinach well in a colander, and let it cool. Chop it, or whirl in a blender until almost puréed. Melt butter in a saucepan, add the flour, and stir well until smooth. Still over heat, slowly add milk and broth, stirring constantly to prevent lumps. Stir in lemon juice and seasonings. Remove saucepan from heat.

Preheat oven to 350°F. Add egg yolks, one at a time, to the sauce, beating well after each addition. Mix in the chopped or puréed spinach. Beat egg whites until stiff, then carefully and thoroughly fold into the spinach mixture (or fold spinach mixture into egg whites if saucepan won't hold it all). Spoon into a buttered 6-cup soufflé dish or casserole, and bake in the preheated oven for 40 minutes. Makes 6 servings.

JOSEPHINE PREMICE

# Sweet Potato Soufflé

2 cups mashed cooked sweet potato
1 ½ cups cream
¾ cup sugar
2 tablespoons butter
1 teaspoon vanilla extract
½ cup sherry wine

juice of 1 orange
grated rind of 1 orange
grated rind of 1 lemon
½ teaspoon salt
5 eggs, separated
butter for baking dish

Preheat oven to 400°F. Put mashed sweet potato in the bowl of an electric mixer, and beat until smooth and fluffy. Add cream, sugar, butter, vanilla, sherry, orange juice, grated rinds and salt, and beat until well mixed. Let everything cool. Beat egg yolks, then stir into the sweet potato mixture. Beat egg whites until stiff and gently fold them into the rest of the mixture. Spoon the batter into a buttered 2-quart soufflé dish or casserole. Bake in the preheated oven for 40 minutes, until soufflé is well puffed up and firm. Makes 10 servings.

This soufflé may be served as a main-dish accompaniment with any poultry, game or pork.

JOAN HURLEY

# Ham and Cheese Soufflé

¼ pound butter (1 stick)
6 eggs, separated
½ pound Parmesan cheese, grated
    (2 cups after grating)
1 cup minced cooked ham
2 tablespoons snipped fresh chives

Preheat oven to 350°F. Cream butter until soft. Add egg yolks, one at a time, beating well after each addition until mixture is light and fluffy. Add grated cheese, ham and chives and mix well. Beat egg whites until stiff and gently fold them into the rest of the mixture. Spoon into a well-buttered 6-cup soufflé dish. Bake in the preheated oven for 30 minutes. Makes 6 servings.

# ANN LANDERS

# Noodle and Spinach Ring

8 ounces medium noodles
salt
10 ounces frozen chopped spinach
butter for mold
⅓ cup bread crumbs
4 ounces American cheese, grated
    (1 cup after grating)
4 eggs
2½ cups milk
1 teaspoon Worcestershire sauce

Cook noodles in 2 quarts water with 1 tablespoon salt until just done; drain. Cook spinach in ½ cup water with ½ teaspoon salt *only* until thawed; drain. Butter a 2-quart ring mold, and in it make alternate layers of noodles, spinach, bread crumbs and cheese, using all of these ingredients. Break eggs into a bowl and add milk, Worcestershire and 1 teaspoon salt. Beat all together until well mixed, then pour into the other ingredients layered in the mold. Set mold in a pan of hot water and slide into a preheated 350°F. oven. Bake for about 45 minutes. Makes 6 servings.

PIA LINDSTROM

# Mushroom and Onion Quiche

8 to 12 mushrooms
3 parsley sprigs
1 medium-size onion
3 tablespoons butter
3 eggs
1 cup light cream
4 ounces Swiss cheese, grated
½ teaspoon salt
¼ teaspoon pepper
9-inch quiche shell, partially baked
    (recipe follows)

Wash and trim mushrooms; roll in a towel to dry. Wash and dry parsley. Peel and quarter onion. Chop all together by hand, or in a food processor. Melt butter and sauté vegetable mixture in it until tender. Mix eggs, cream, cheese and seasonings until well blended. Combine with mushroom mixture, and pour all into the partially baked shell. Bake in a preheated 375°F. oven for 35 to 40 minutes. Let the quiche cool before serving. Makes 6 servings.

## Pâté Brisée for Quiche Shell

1⅓ cups flour
1 teaspoon salt
¼ pound butter (1 stick)
2 to 3 tablespoons ice water

Mix everything in a food processor. Or sift flour and salt together into a bowl, cut in the butter until the mixture looks like cornmeal, then add just enough of the ice water to make the ingredients hold together. Either way, pat dough into a ball and roll out on a lightly floured board to a circle about 11 inches around. Roll onto the pin and gently unroll on a 9-inch quiche pan or pie tin. Fit the dough into the pan without stretching; trim around the edge leaving ½ inch extra all around. Fold the extra dough under, and crimp or flute it. Line the pastry with foil and weights (dried beans, etc.), and bake in a preheated 400°F. oven for 10 minutes. Remove weights and foil and continue to bake for 10 minutes longer, until pastry is golden. Cool before filling. Makes one 9-inch shell.

34

# ELIZABETH TAYLOR

# Quiche Lorraine

pastry for 1-crust, 9-inch pie
5 slices of bacon
12 ounces American cheese
½ cup light cream
1 tablespoon arrowroot
1 cup milk
¼ teaspoon salt
¼ teaspoon pepper
5 eggs
¼ teaspoon cayenne pepper

Preheat oven to 400°F. Roll out pastry to a thin sheet and line a 9-inch pie pan or an 8-inch-square pan with removable bottom. Bring the pastry high up on the sides all around and crimp or flute the edges. Fry bacon until crisp, and crumble; set aside. Grate the cheese. Pour cream into a large bowl and stir in arrowroot until well mixed. Slowly add milk, then salt, pepper, grated cheese and crumbled bacon. Stir to mix. In a separate bowl, beat eggs until light, then add to cheese mixture and beat all together well. Pour into the pastry-lined pan and sprinkle with cayenne. Bake in the preheated oven for 45 minutes. Cut into small wedges or squares and serve hot. Makes 6 to 8 servings.
*Variations:* Add sautéed chopped mushrooms; omit bacon and add chopped cooked shrimps, lobster or crab meat.

# 4

# FISH AND SHELLFISH

## HIS EXCELLENCY ANWAR EL-SADAT

# Baked Fish

Dress and scale a large whole fish, 6 to 8 pounds (whitefish, red snapper, striped bass). Do not detach the head, but remove the eyes. Peel and mince 4 or 5 large white onions. Put plenty of butter with a little oil or fat in a baking dish large enough to hold the fish. Add onions and bake in a preheated 350°F. oven until browned; stir onions occasionally so they brown evenly. While onions brown, make a mixture of chopped parsley, chopped green peppers, chopped tomatoes and dry bread crumbs, seasoned with salt, pepper and ground ginger, and all mixed with nobs of butter. Spread a thick coating of this inside and outside the dressed fish.

When onions are golden brown, lift baking dish from the oven and lay the fish carefully on the onions. Return to the oven and bake for 20 minutes, or until fish is done to your taste. During baking, baste the fish 4 or 5 times with liquid from the bottom of the pan. Carefully remove baked fish to a hot serving dish. Drain off fat from baking dish. Make a thick sauce with onions and juices remaining in the pan; add a little white stock, if desired, to give the consistency you want. Spoon over the fish, and garnish with lemon slices and parsley bouquets. Serve very hot, arranging each portion on a bed of boiled white rice. Makes 6 servings.

# SHIRLEY BASSEY

# Redfish Supreme

1 redfish (red drum or channel bass),
    5 pounds
salt and pepper
½ cup oil
⅜ pound butter (1½ sticks)
6 tablespoons flour
2 tablespoons chopped green onions
    (scallions)
1 cup chopped celery
½ cup chopped parsley
½ teaspoon crushed red pepper
½ pound mushrooms, chopped
2 dozen oysters, shelled

1 pound fresh shrimps, shelled and
    deveined
½ cup grated cheese
½ cup dry bread crumbs

Dress the fish. Mix 1 teaspoon salt and 1 teaspoon pepper with the oil, and rub fish inside and outside with all of the mixture. Place fish on a rack in a roasting pan, and pour 1 cup water under the rack (fish must not touch water). Cover the pan and bake in a preheated 400°F. oven for 30 minutes. Pour off drippings and reserve. Keep fish warm.

Melt 1 stick of butter in a large skillet and add the flour. Cook over low heat, stirring constantly, until flour is golden brown. Add green onions, celery, parsley and red pepper. Cook for 10 minutes. Add reserved fish drippings and enough water to make a thick sauce. Season with salt and pepper to taste. Melt remaining butter in a separate saucepan and sauté mushrooms until tender. Transfer fish to a large flat baking dish about 4 inches deep. Spoon the sauce over it, then arrange sautéed mushrooms, oysters and shrimps on top. Sprinkle grated cheese, then bread crumbs over all. Bake in the 400°F. oven for about 30 minutes, until everything is well browned and bubbly. Makes 8 servings.

# MARION ANDERSON

# Flounder Roulades

2 ounces butter
1 teaspoon salt
dash of pepper
pinch of dried basil
1 pound flounder fillets, about 4 fillets
½ cup dry bread crumbs
paprika

Preheat oven to 350°F. Melt butter and mix in salt, pepper and basil. Wipe fillets with a damp paper towel. Dip each one into the butter mixture, then into the crumbs. Roll up each fillet tightly and secure with a wooden food pick or small stainless-steel skewer. Arrange roulades in a baking dish that will just hold them. Pour any remaining butter over them, and sprinkle with paprika. Bake for 25 to 30 minutes, until fish flakes easily when tested with a fork. Makes 2 servings.

# WILLIS REED

## Casserole of Calico Bass, Shrimps and Crab

1 pound crab meat
1 pound fresh shrimps, shelled and
    deveined
2 tablespoons butter
1 onion, grated
1 garlic clove, minced
2 tablespoons flour
½ cup chopped mushrooms
1 cup white wine
½ cup milk

1 tablespoon Worcestershire sauce
1 tablespoon chopped fresh parsley
½ teaspoon prepared horseradish
¼ teaspoon dry mustard
¼ teaspoon dried tarragon
dash of hot sauce
salt and pepper
2 pounds fillets of calico bass
butter for casserole and top
⅔ cup cracker crumbs

Pick over crab meat and remove any bits of cartilage. Split each shrimp into halves. Melt butter in a large heavy pot over low heat, and in it sauté onion and garlic until onion is tender. Add flour and mushrooms, mix well, then blend in the wine, milk, Worcestershire, parsley, horseradish, dry mustard, tarragon and the dash of hot sauce. Cook over low heat, stirring constantly, until the mixture forms a creamy sauce. Season with salt and pepper to taste. Add bass fillets and uncooked shrimp halves. Cook over very low heat for 15 minutes; if mixture becomes too thick, add a little more milk. Fold in crab meat. Spoon mixture into a well-buttered 3-quart casserole, and sprinkle top with cracker crumbs. Dot with butter. Bake uncovered in a preheated 350°F. oven for 1 hour. Makes 10 servings.

## THE HONORABLE
## PERCY E. SUTTON

# Baked
# Red Snapper
# with Party Sauce

1 whole red snapper, 6 pounds
½ cup flour
salt and pepper
3 ounces butter
2 onions, minced
1 garlic clove, minced
½ pound fresh mushrooms, chopped
½ cup chopped green pepper
2 cups chopped celery
4 cups tomato sauce

| | |
|---|---|
| 1 tablespoon Worcestershire sauce | 1 lemon, sliced thin, with seeds removed |
| 1 tablespoon ketchup | 1 cup white wine |
| 1 teaspoon chili powder | 2 bay leaves |
| ½ teaspoon Tabasco | ½ cup chopped fresh parsley |

Dress the fish. Season flour with salt and pepper and dredge fish inside and out-side with the seasoned flour. Place fish in a large baking dish. Melt butter in a large skillet, and in it sauté onions, garlic, mushrooms, green pepper and celery, covered, until tender. Put tomato sauce, Worcestershire, ketchup, chili powder, Tabasco and half of the lemon slices in a blender container, and whirl until smooth. Add to sautéed vegetables, mix well, then stir in the wine and add bay leaves. Pour the sauce around the fish. Bake in a preheated 350°F. oven for 1 hour, basting often with the sauce. Garnish with remaining lemon slices and the chopped parsley. Makes 6 servings.

# THE HONORABLE ANDREW YOUNG

# Seafood from the Bayou

1 pound fresh shrimps in shells
1 pound fresh crayfish in shells
1 pound shelled crab meat
1 pint shelled oysters with liquor
1 bunch of green onions (scallions)
¼ pound butter (1 stick)
½ cup minced celery
1 cup cream
½ cup flour
1 teaspoon seafood seasoning
    (mixture of cayenne pepper and salt)
1 teaspoon Worcestershire sauce

Rinse shrimps, shell and devein. Wash crayfish, separate heads from tails, and shell tails. Pick over crab meat and remove any bits of cartilage. Check oysters for any bits of shell. Trim and chop green onions. Melt butter in a large skillet. Add green onions and celery and sauté until wilted. Add shrimps and crayfish tails and cook for 5 minutes. Add crab meat, oysters and oyster liquor. Cook for 10 minutes longer. Mix cream with flour and stir into shellfish. Cook and stir over low heat until thickened. Stir in seasoning. Serve over freshly cooked pasta. Makes 6 servings.

# Shrimps au Gratin

1 pound fresh raw shrimps in shells
2 cups Béchamel Sauce (recipe follows)
½ cup grated Gruyère cheese
2 tablespoons ketchup
½ teaspoon chili sauce,
    or 2 or 3 drops of Tabasco
¼ cup mixed grated Gruyère and
    Jack cheese, approximately
¼ cup fresh bread crumbs, approximately

Cover shrimps with water, bring to a boil, then simmer for about 5 minutes, until pink but barely cooked. At once cool with cold water, and shell and devein shrimps. Make Béchamel sauce, and stir in ½ cup cheese, the ketchup, and chili sauce or Tabasco; mix thoroughly.

Reheat shrimps by pouring boiling water over them for 1 minute; drain. Arrange shrimps in a shallow gratin dish, and spoon sauce over them. Sprinkle with cheese and bread crumbs, the amounts to your taste. Slide under the broiler for 5 to 10 minutes, until crumbs and cheese are golden. Makes 4 servings.

## Béchamel Sauce

1¾ cups milk
3 tablespoons chopped onion
3 tablespoons grated carrot
1 tablespoon chopped parsley stems
1 bay leaf
1 whole clove
3 ounces butter
4 tablespoons flour
½ cup chicken broth
½ teaspoon salt
pinch of white pepper
pinch of grated nutmeg

Pour milk into a saucepan and add onion, carrot, parsley stems, bay leaf and the whole clove. Simmer over very low heat, or on an asbestos pad, or in the top part

44

of a double boiler set over boiling water, for about 10 minutes; do not let milk boil. Remove the pan from the heat.

Melt the butter in a 1-quart saucepan until foamy. Remove pan from heat and stir in the flour. Stir in chicken broth and mix well. Return saucepan to low heat and strain the flavored milk into the mixture, stirring constantly with a wooden spoon or paddle until everything is mixed. Let the sauce simmer for 10 minutes, stirring often, until there is no taste of raw flour and sauce is smooth and thick. Add salt, pepper and nutmeg. Keep sauce warm over hot water until you are ready to use it. Makes 2 cups sauce.

# BARRY MANILOW

# Spaghetti with White Clam Sauce

4 pounds fresh hardshell clams
½ cup oil
1 onion, chopped fine
2 garlic cloves, peeled and minced
1 celery rib, minced
½ cup white wine
2 tablespoons chopped parsley
1 tablespoon minced fresh basil
½ teaspoon dried orégano
salt
½ cup pine nuts, chopped fine
black pepper
½ cup heavy cream

1 pound pasta (spaghetti, fettuccine, etc.)
butter (optional)
½ cup freshly grated Parmesan
   or Romano cheese

Arrange clams in a single layer in a large pan and cover with cold water. Let them stand for several hours, or longer. Scrub shells thoroughly. Place clams in a steamer over 1½ inches of water and steam just until the shells open. At once remove from heat. Remove clams from shells, and pour the liquid in the steamer through a fine strainer lined with moistened cloth. Save the strained broth. Chop the clams.

Heat oil in a skillet over moderate heat. Add onion, garlic and celery, cover, and let vegetables cook for at least 10 minutes. Add ½ cup of the strained clam broth, the wine, herbs and ¼ teaspoon salt. Add pine nuts and liberal amounts of freshly ground pepper. Cover and cook over low heat for 30 minutes. Add clams and cook for 10 minutes longer. Add cream just before serving.

While clam sauce is being cooked, bring a large kettle of water to a boil, then add 2 tablespoons salt and the pasta. Cook until *al dente,* then drain and add a dot of butter, or add butter to individual servings. Spoon clam sauce on top and serve cheese separately. Makes 8 servings.

JOSÉ QUINTERO

# Spaghetti with Panamanian Cold Shrimp Sauce

2 pounds fresh raw shrimps in shells
salt
2 cups mayonnaise
1 medium-size onion, peeled and minced
4 garlic cloves, peeled
1 fresh hot chili pepper,
    cut into very small pieces
4 drops of fresh lime juice
2 drops of Worcestershire sauce
oil
1 pound spaghetti
2 ounces butter, melted
4 ounces Parmesan cheese, grated
    (1 cup after grating)

Cook shrimps in lightly salted water for 5 minutes. Drain immediately, and cool. When shrimps are cool, shell and devein them. Put mayonnaise into a bowl large enough to hold shrimps and sauce. Add onion, and push garlic through a press into mayonnaise. Add chili pepper, lime juice and Worcestershire, and mix well. Fold in the shrimps, cover the bowl, and refrigerate the sauce for 12 to 24 hours.

Bring a large kettle of water to a boil. Add a few drops of oil and 2 tablespoons salt. Drop in spaghetti and cook for 6 to 8 minutes. Drain pasta, and mix in melted butter and grated cheese. Arrange pasta on a large serving platter, and spoon cold shrimp sauce on top. Serve immediately. Makes 6 servings.

## MRS. JOANNE CUMMINGS

# Lobster Amandine

½ cup crosswise ½-inch pieces
    of Pascal celery
½ cup 1-inch squares of fresh green pepper
½ pound fresh mushrooms, sliced
6 tablespoons peanut oil
½ cup cooked lobster meat
½ cup snow peas, each cut diagonally
    into 2 pieces
½ cup thin slices of water chestnuts
3 tablespoons 1-inch squares of pimiento
½ tablespoon salt
¼ teaspoon black pepper
¼ teaspoon garlic salt

¼ teaspoon monosodium glutamate
1½ tablespoons cornstarch
¾ cup cool chicken stock
15 to 20 blanched whole almonds,
    toasted and salted

Drop celery pieces into a small amount of hot water, cover, and cook for about 5 minutes; drain. Cook green pepper in the same way for 1 minute; drain. Sauté sliced mushrooms in 2 tablespoons of the oil for 2 or 3 minutes; drain. Heat remaining oil in a large saucepan or wok and drop in lobster, snow peas, water chestnuts, celery, green pepper, mushrooms and pimiento. Cook over moderately high heat for 5 minutes. Add seasonings, blend well, and cook for 2 minutes longer. Stir cornstarch into chicken stock until completely dissolved, and pour into the lobster mixture. Cover pan and cook for 6 minutes. If sauce appears too thick, add a little more stock. Heap on a serving dish and sprinkle top with almonds. Serve at once with Cantonese fried rice. Makes 2 large or 3 medium-size servings.

PERLE MESTA

# Seafood Newburg
# in Crêpes

3 cups seafood (crab, lobster, shrimp)
3 ounces butter
½ cup sherry wine
⅓ cup flour
½ teaspoon salt

½ teaspoon Tabasco
1 tablespoon Escoffier sauce
2 cups light cream
2 egg yolks
18 Crêpes (recipe follows)

Pick over shellfish, remove any bits of cartilage or shell, and cut shellfish into bite-size pieces. Melt half of the butter in a heavy skillet. Add seafood pieces and sherry, and simmer for 10 minutes. In another saucepan melt remaining butter. Stir in flour, salt, Tabasco and Escoffier sauce until smooth. With a wire whisk gradually stir in the cream. Cook over low heat, stirring constantly, until sauce is thick. Stir part of the hot sauce into the egg yolks, beat well, then stir egg yolks into the rest of the sauce and cook for just a few minutes. Gently mix in the seafood.

Spoon about ¼ cup of the seafood mixture into each crêpe, then roll up. Arrange filled crêpes, seam sides down, on 1 or 2 shallow oven-to-table dishes. Spoon remaining sauce down the center of the rolled crêpes. Bake in a preheated 325°F. oven until very hot. Serve at once. Makes 6 servings, 3 crêpes each.

## Crêpes

1 cup sifted flour
2 tablespoons sugar
½ teaspoon salt

1 cup milk
3 eggs
butter for frying

Sift flour, sugar and salt together. Beat milk and eggs together, then beat liquid mixture into dry ingredients, beating or stirring until the batter is satin smooth. Strain the batter.

Heat an 8-inch skillet or crêpe pan. With a wad of paper toweling, rub the bottom of the pan with just enough butter to coat it evenly. Pour 3 tablespoons of the batter into the skillet and at once tilt the pan to all sides so batter spreads out and fills the entire pan with a thin layer of batter. Cook until the crêpe is brown on the bottom, which happens quickly, then turn over and brown the other side. Remove the finished crêpe to a layer of paper towel to drain. Again brush the pan with butter and continue to cook the crêpes until all the batter is used. Makes 18 to 24 crêpes.

# Seafood Ile de France

3 lobsters, 1 ½ pounds each, cooked
2 cups fresh or frozen crab meat
1 tablespoon olive oil
2 tablespoons chopped shallots or onion
1 garlic clove, peeled and crushed
1 can (35 ounces) tomatoes
1 tablespoon minced fresh tarragon,
    or ½ tablespoon dried
1 tablespoon minced fresh chervil,
    or ½ tablespoon dried
3 tablespoons butter
3 tablespoons flour
1 cup milk
¼ cup heavy cream
¾ teaspoon salt
dash of black pepper
dash of grated nutmeg
¼ cup Pernod (optional)

Remove lobster meat from shells and cut into bite-size pieces. Pick over crab meat and remove any bits of cartilage. Prepare *sauce américaine:* Heat olive oil in a large saucepan and sauté shallots and garlic until golden. Add tomatoes, tarragon and chervil. Simmer, uncovered, until reduced to about 1 ½ cups. Purée through a food mill or in an electric blender, then strain to remove tomato seeds.

Prepare cream sauce: Melt butter in a saucepan, stir in flour until smooth, then add milk, cream and seasonings. Cook and stir until sauce is smooth and thickened. Mix the two sauces together and transfer to the top part of a large double boiler. Mix in lobster and crab meat, and add Pernod if you like. Heat, stirring occasionally. Serve in scallop shells. Makes 6 to 8 servings.

# THE HONORABLE EDMUND G. BROWN, JR.

# Paella Amigos

1 lobster, 1½ pounds
6 Cherrystone clams
6 mussels
½ pound crab meat
1 frying chicken, about 3 pounds
¼ pound boneless veal
¼ pound boneless lean pork
1 pound ripe tomatoes, about 2
1 sweet red pepper
2 garlic cloves
1 medium-size onion
¼ cup olive oil
2 teaspoons salt
¼ teaspoon freshly ground pepper
2 cups uncooked rice

4 cups water
10 ounces frozen peas
9 ounces frozen artichoke hearts
1 teaspoon whole saffron
12 asparagus tips
2 pimientos

Remove meat from the lobster. Scrub clams and mussels. Pick over crab and remove any bits of cartilage. Cut chicken into 8 meaty parts (neck, back pieces and wing tips can be set aside for stock). Dice veal and pork. Peel and chop tomatoes. Wash red pepper, remove ribs and seeds, and chop pepper. Peel and mince 1 garlic clove and the onion. Heat the oil in a large, heavy deep skillet. Add chicken, veal and pork, and cook until chicken pieces are browned on all sides. Add garlic and onion and cook, stirring, until onion is translucent. Add salt, pepper and chopped tomatoes; cover skillet and cook for 10 minutes. Mix in rice and 4 cups water; stir well to combine. Add chopped red pepper, peas and artichoke hearts. Cover skillet again and cook over low heat for about 20 minutes.

Peel remaining garlic clove and in a mortar mash it with the saffron. Add to the paella, and with a large spoon turn rice from top to bottom to mix well. Add crab meat and lobster meat, cover, and cook for 10 to 15 minutes longer.

Meanwhile, put mussels and clams in a heavy pot with ½ cup water. Cover pot, bring water to a lively boil over high heat, and cook for 2 minutes, until all shells open. Cook asparagus in boiling salted water until tender; drain. (Or heat canned asparagus tips.) Cut pimientos into strips.

Arrange rice in a shallow paella pan or a large shallow casserole. Place open mussels and clams in their shells on top of the rice, and garnish with asparagus tips and pimiento strips. Makes 6 servings.

51

JOHN LOUIS WILSON, A.I.A.

# Louisiana Jambalaya

2 tablespoons oil
1 cup chopped onions
1 garlic clove, peeled and minced
½ pound salt pork, chopped
1 pound hot Italian sausages, chopped
1 slice of cooked ham, chopped
1 green pepper, chopped fine
½ cup chopped sweet red pepper
2 cups chopped celery
1 bunch of green onions (scallions),
    chopped fine
½ cup chopped fresh parsley
1 teaspoon dried thyme
4 bay leaves, crumbled
4 cups water

4 cups fish stock or clam broth
1 can (35 ounces) tomatoes
1 teaspoon salt
1 quart shelled oysters with liquor
5 cups uncooked rice
5 pounds raw fresh shrimps,
    shelled and deveined
2 pounds bay scallops

Heat the oil in a large heavy Dutch oven or kettle, about 6-quart size. Stir in onions, garlic, salt pork, hot sausages and ham. Cover the kettle and cook until fat from the meats has been rendered and onions are wilted. Add green and red peppers, celery, green onions, the herbs, water, fish stock, canned tomatoes and salt. Drain oysters in a large sieve set in a bowl, and add the drained oyster liquor to the kettle. Mix well, then add rice and cook very gently, stirring all the while, for 10 minutes. Add shrimps, scallops and oysters. Cook over low heat, stirring from the bottom to prevent scorching, for 45 minutes. Serve Worcestershire sauce and Tabasco as accompaniments. Makes 25 servings.

# 5

## POULTRY AND GAME BIRDS

# Chicken Continental

10 ounces frozen broccoli
salt
butter for casserole
2 ounces butter
4 tablespoons flour
1 cup chicken broth
½ cup light cream
½ cup Sauterne wine
1 teaspoon Worcestershire sauce
pepper
½ cup grated American cheese (2 ounces)
2 cups cut-up cooked chicken
grated Parmesan cheese

Cook broccoli in ½ cup water with ½ teaspoon salt until just tender, but not mushy. Pour off cooking water, and save it. Drain broccoli well, then arrange it in a buttered 6-cup casserole. Melt 2 ounces butter, stir in flour, then add chicken broth and cream and enough of the broccoli cooking water to make a smooth thick sauce. Cook over low heat, stirring, until sauce is well blended. Add wine, Worcestershire, and salt and pepper to taste, then stir in the American cheese. Do not cook sauce after cheese is added.

Arrange chicken pieces on top of broccoli, pour the sauce over everything, and sprinkle the top lavishly with grated Parmesan cheese. Bake in a preheated 400°F. oven for 20 minutes, or until top is golden brown and sauce bubbly. Makes 4 servings.

# MIKE DOUGLAS

# Chicken Parmigiana

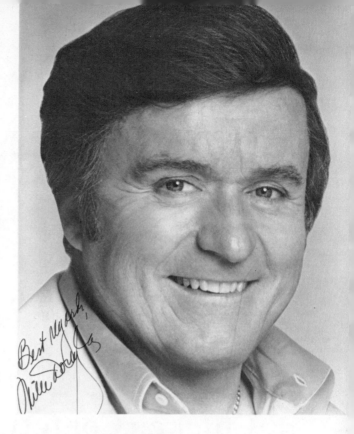

1 large frying chicken, 3½ pounds
salt and freshly ground pepper
2 ounces butter or olive oil
1 cup sliced mushrooms
1 green pepper, cored, seeded and chopped
½ cup chopped onion
1 garlic clove, peeled and minced
2 cups chopped, peeled and seeded
    tomatoes
½ cup dry vermouth

½ cup sliced stuffed olives
¼ cup freshly grated Parmesan cheese

Preheat oven to 350°F. Cut chicken into serving pieces, and sprinkle with salt and pepper. Melt butter in a large shallow casserole, and brown the chicken pieces in it. Sprinkle in the mushrooms and cook for 5 minutes. Add green pepper, onion, garlic, tomatoes and vermouth. Cover casserole tightly and transfer to the oven. Bake for 30 minutes. Add olives and bake for 10 minutes longer. Sprinkle cheese on top and serve. Makes 4 servings.

GOLDA MEIR

# Chicken Confetti

3 frying chickens, about 3 pounds each
1 cup flour
2 tablespoons salt
1 teaspoon dried thyme
½ teaspoon poultry seasoning
½ cup melted chicken fat or oil
1 cup orange juice

1 cup clear chicken consommé
½ cup dry sherry wine
2 cans (10 ounces each) artichoke hearts
½ pound mushrooms, washed and trimmed
2 red onions, peeled and sliced
1 cup slivered pitted olives
coarsely ground ginger

Cut chickens into quarters. In a bowl or paper bag mix flour, salt, thyme and poultry seasoning. Coat chicken pieces with the mixture. Heat fat or oil in a large skillet and brown chicken pieces lightly. Transfer pieces to a 3-quart casserole, and pour in orange juice, consommé and sherry. Simmer for 5 minutes. Transfer to a preheated 350°F. oven, and bake for 1 hour, occasionally basting with the liquids.

Meanwhile, open cans of artichoke hearts and pour hearts and the liquid into a saucepan. Add mushrooms, and steam together until mushrooms are tender. Pour vegetables into the casserole, then spread red onion slices and slivered olives on top. Sprinkle ginger all over the chicken. Continue baking for 45 minutes longer. Serve with white rice. Makes 12 servings.

# VIVIENNE W. NEARING

# Chicken with Orange

4 whole chicken breasts
flour
salt and pepper
ground ginger
2 tablespoons butter
2 tablespoons corn oil
6 ounces frozen orange-juice concentrate
6 tablespoons water
1 large Jaffa orange, or other tart orange
4 to 6 ounces Cointreau
    or Grand Marnier liqueur

Split chicken breasts, remove skin and bones, and wipe with a damp cloth. Mix about ⅔ cup flour with salt, pepper and ground ginger to taste, and dust the 8 chicken pieces with the mixture. Heat butter and corn oil in a large heavy skillet (preferably copper-bottomed), and brown chicken on skin side, then turn over and brown on the bone side. Add orange-juice concentrate and water, cover the skillet, and simmer for 10 minutes.

Cut the orange into 8 thin slices. (Use 2 oranges if yours is not large enough.) Place 1 orange slice on each chicken piece, and add the liqueur to the pan. Cover skillet and steam for 5 minutes longer. Adjust the sauce by adding more liqueur or water if needed. Slide the skillet under the broiler for 5 minutes to brown the oranges. Serve on a bed of rice. Makes 8 servings.

ARTHUR ASHE

# Virginia Fried Chicken with Peas and Rice

1 frying chicken, 3 pounds
1 cup milk
2 tablespoons Tabasco
1 tablespoon salt
1 teaspoon freshly ground black pepper

1 teaspoon grated nutmeg
juice of ½ lemon
1 pound lard, or 2 cups oil and
    ¼ pound butter
1 cup flour

Cut chicken into 8 pieces (save neck and back pieces for stock), and wash well. Place in a mixing bowl and add milk, Tabasco, salt, pepper and nutmeg. Turn chicken in the mixture, and let it stand in the refrigerator for a few hours. Overnight is even better. Add lemon juice to chicken.

Heat lard, or oil and butter, in a large heavy skillet. Lift chicken from milk mixture and transfer to another bowl with the flour. Add more flour if necessary to coat the chicken pieces on all sides. Turn heat high under the skillet and cook chicken, skin side down, until it is a warm brown. Turn pieces over with tongs, reduce heat to medium, and continue to cook for 20 to 30 minutes, until chicken is golden brown all over and cooked through. Drain well on paper toweling. Arrange pieces around a mound of peas and rice (recipe follows). Makes 8 servings.

## Peas and Rice

2 cups dried black-eyed peas
1 pound salt pork, cubed
7 cups water
5 slices of bacon
2 medium-size onions, peeled and chopped
3 garlic cloves, peeled and minced
1 tablespoon Worcestershire sauce

1 cup tomato sauce
1 cup chopped green pepper
½ cup minced fresh parsley
1 bay leaf, crumbled
dash of cayenne pepper
1½ cups uncooked rice

Soak dried peas in cold water for 2 hours. Drain, and transfer peas to a 4-quart pot. Add salt pork and 4 cups water. Cook uncovered for 45 minutes. Fry bacon in a large skillet until crisp. Remove bacon to absorbent paper to drain. In the

bacon fat remaining in the pan cook the onions, garlic and Worcestershire over low heat for about 20 minutes. Spoon into peas, add tomato sauce and 3 cups water, and cook for 1 hour longer. Add green pepper, parsley, bay leaf, cayenne and last the rice. Cook over low heat for 30 minutes longer, until peas and rice are tender. Crumble bacon slices and add to the peas and rice last. Spoon on a large platter in a mound and surround with chicken pieces. Makes 8 servings.

## MME RUTH DUBONNET

# Poulet Véronique

1 teaspoon celery salt
½ tablespoon salt
½ cup flour
8 single chicken breasts, boned and skinned
3 tablespoons oil
1½ cups red wine
½ cup chicken broth
2 teaspoons dried rosemary
1 teaspoon dried tarragon
¼ teaspoon peppercorns
½ pound seedless green grapes

Mix celery salt, salt and flour. Dip chicken into seasoned flour; reserve remaining flour. Heat oil in a Dutch oven and in it brown chicken pieces on both sides. Sprinkle remaining flour over chicken and stir in wine and chicken broth. Combine rosemary, tarragon and peppercorns on a square of muslin, and tie up with string to form an herb bag. Add herb bag to chicken. Bring liquids to a boil, cover, and place the pot in a preheated 350°F. oven. Bake for 45 minutes.

Wash grapes, remove all stems, and roll in a towel to dry thoroughly. Stir grapes into the chicken pot and let stand for 5 minutes. Arrange chicken breasts on a bed of rice. Discard herb bag, and spoon grape sauce over chicken. Makes 6 servings with extras.

# Chicken in a Pot

*"Be careful in selecting the ingredients for this dish, since they are undisguised by sauces or heavy seasoning. For symmetry the vegetables should be all about the same size. Take time to truss the chicken neatly, as it will be easier to brown," says Mrs. Susskind.*

1 roasting chicken or capon, 5 pounds
2 ounces butter
¼ cup dry white wine
½ cup chicken broth
12 small new red potatoes, unpeeled
18 baby carrots, peeled
18 small white onions, peeled
12 medium-size mushrooms, cut into
    halves
¼ teaspoon crumbled dried rosemary
½ cup chopped celery leaves
salt and pepper
monosodium glutamate (optional)

Truss the chicken: sew up the cavity, tie the legs together, and tie wings under the bird. Melt the butter in a large skillet and brown the chicken slowly for about 30 minutes. Keep turning the bird to brown it evenly on all sides. Transfer chicken to a large casserole or roasting pan. Pour wine and broth into the skillet and bring to a boil, stirring to deglaze the skillet. Pour this mixture over the chicken, cover, and cook over medium heat for 45 minutes.

Add vegetables in layers, potatoes on the bottom, then carrots, then onions, finally mushrooms. Sprinkle rosemary and celery leaves on top. Cover casserole again and cook for 45 minutes longer, or until chicken is tender and vegetables are done. Place chicken on an extra large platter, remove trussing strings, and arrange all the vegetables around the bird. Fill a sauceboat with pan juices, and moisten each serving with a little of the juices. Correct the seasoning with salt and pepper if you like. A light sprinkling of monosodium glutamate enhances the vegetables. Makes 6 servings.

## THE HONORABLE CHARLES B. RANGEL

# Chicken Pilau

1 ½ cups uncooked rice
2 ounces butter
2 onions, peeled and cut into thin slices
2 garlic cloves, peeled and minced
2 broiling chickens, 1 ½ pounds each
2 teaspoons salt
1 teaspoon curry powder
½ teaspoon ground ginger
2 cups plain yogurt
2 cups chicken broth

Wash rice in several waters and drain well. Melt butter in a 2 ½-quart casserole or Dutch oven. Sauté onions and garlic for 10 minutes, stirring frequently. Quarter the chickens and add to the casserole; brown on all sides. Add salt, curry powder, ginger, yogurt and broth; mix well. Pour in the rice; the liquid should just cover it; if not, add a little water. Bring to a boil, cover tightly, and cook over low heat for 35 minutes, or until chicken and rice are tender. Makes 8 servings.

MRS. WILLIAM V. S. TUBMAN

# Chicken and Groundnut Stew

1 chicken, 3 to 3½ pounds
salt and pepper
1 large onion, peeled and sliced
4 to 6 cups water
½ pound fresh mushrooms,
    trimmed and chopped
4 to 6 hard-cooked eggs, shelled
2 cups freshly roasted groundnuts
    (peanuts)

Cut up chicken, wash well, and season with salt and pepper. Place in a large saucepan, add onion, and pour in enough water just to cover chicken. Bring to a boil and simmer as if you were making a soup until chicken is about half done. Pour off the chicken broth into another container. Add mushrooms and eggs to chicken, and adjust seasoning to taste.

Make groundnut stock: Shell peanuts, then grind in a food grinder or mortar. Transfer to a pan and add some of the chicken broth. Mix well, and strain into the container of broth. Again mix well, then strain into the saucepan of chicken. Cook over medium heat until the mixture becomes thick. Serve over boiled rice. Makes 4 to 6 servings.

Peanut butter, crunchy or creamy, can be used in place of the fresh peanuts, but fresh nuts give a better flavor. If crunchy peanut butter is used, strain mixture of broth and peanut butter.

PRINCESS
IRENE GALITZINE

# Chicken Roll (Kournik) with Supreme Sauce

## Pastry

2¼ cups flour
pinch of salt
½ pound butter (2 sticks)
1 cake compressed fresh yeast
4 raw egg yolks

Sift flour and salt together. Cut in butter until bits are tiny. Add yeast and egg yolks and mix well. Set pastry aside to rise while preparing chicken filling.

## Chicken Filling

2 stewing chickens, about 6 pounds each
3 cups chopped fresh mushrooms
6 hard-cooked eggs, shelled
½ pound butter (2 sticks)
1½ cups cooked rice
2 teaspoons salt
1 teaspoon pepper

Dress and draw chickens. Cut them into pieces and put in a large heavy kettle. Cover with water and simmer for 3 hours, or until chicken is tender. Strain the broth and reserve for sauce (recipe follows). Remove skin and bones from chicken and cut meat into small pieces. Simmer mushrooms in a little water until just tender, 5 to 10 minutes. Chop eggs in pieces about the size of mushroom pieces. Melt butter in a large skillet and add chicken, mushrooms, rice and eggs. Cook, stirring, until mixture is lightly browned. Season with salt and pepper.

Roll out the pastry on a lightly floured board to a rectangular sheet no thicker than standard piecrust. Spread chicken mixture evenly over the pastry, leaving space along all the edges. Roll up the pastry, in jelly-roll fashion, to make a fat

64

cylinder. Place seam side down in a greased baking dish. Bake in a preheated 400°F. oven for 20 minutes. Slice to serve, and accompany with Supreme Sauce. Makes 12 servings.

## Supreme Sauce

6 ounces butter
4 tablespoons flour
3 cups chicken broth
3 egg yolks
salt and pepper

Melt butter in a saucepan. Off the heat stir in the flour. Over low heat stir in as much of the chicken broth as needed to make a sauce as thick as you like. Beat egg yolks well, stir in a little of the hot sauce to warm them, then off the heat stir the egg-yolk mixture into the balance of the sauce, stirring all the while. Serve at once, over slices of *kournik*. Makes about 4 cups.

NATHAN CUMMINGS

# Chicken
# à la Cummings

1 pound chicken breasts
2 tablespoons salad oil
1 tablespoon lemon juice
2 tablespoons grated Parmesan cheese
1 sliver of garlic
¼ teaspoon dried orégano

1 teaspoon salt
½ teaspoon black pepper
½ cup flour
½ tablespoon paprika
3 ounces butter
½ cup water or chicken stock

If chicken breasts are whole, split them. Rinse and pat dry. Mix oil, lemon juice, 1 tablespoon of the cheese, the garlic, orégano, and half of salt and pepper. Beat with a rotary egg beater for 1 minute. Pour at once over chicken pieces in a glass or ceramic container, and refrigerate for 2 hours or longer. Turn breasts over several times.

Make noodles, but do not cook them, and make the sauce while the chicken is marinating.

Sift together the flour, paprika, remaining salt, pepper and Parmesan cheese. Remove chicken from marinade and coat pieces completely with the flour mixture. Melt 2 ounces of the butter in a skillet and sauté chicken over moderate heat until browned on both sides. Place pieces on a rack with a drip pan underneath, and bake in a preheated 350°F. oven for 35 to 45 minutes. After a few minutes, pour water or stock into the drip pan to prevent scorching. Add more liquid if necessary. During last 10 minutes drizzle remaining butter, melted, over chicken. Serve in the center of truffled noodles (recipe follows), and spoon chicken and mushroom sauce (recipe follows) over all. Makes 2 servings.

## Truffled Noodles

2 cups flour
salt
4 egg yolks
4 to 6 tablespoons hot water
2 quarts boiling water

¼ pound butter (1 stick), cut into 8 slices
freshly ground black pepper
⅔ cup light cream
4 ounces Parmesan cheese, freshly grated
2 large white Italian truffles, sliced

Sift flour and ½ teaspoon salt together onto a board. Make a well in the center and drop in the egg yolks. Gradually work the egg yolks into the flour, adding the

66

hot water as necessary, to make a stiff dough. Knead dough until smooth. Cut dough into 2 portions and roll out each half on a floured board to a paper-thin sheet. Let the sheets dry for 15 to 20 minutes.

Fold the sheets of dough into rolls. With a very sharp long knife, cut the rolls crosswise into ½-inch-wide strips. Toss noodles gently with the fingers to unfold them. Spread noodles on a floured board and cover them with a towel. Let them stand for no longer than 1 hour.

Cook noodles in the boiling water with 1 tablespoon salt for 3 or 4 minutes. Drain and transfer to a dry pan. Gently heat noodles while adding the butter slices and pepper to taste. Add the cream and let it heat thoroughly, tossing once or twice, until most of the cream has been absorbed. Add the grated cheese and sliced truffles. Heat, still tossing gently, until noodles are evenly coated with cheese, 2 or 3 minutes. Turn out immediately on a serving dish, make a well in the center, and arrange chicken breasts in the center.

## Chicken and Mushroom Sauce

1¼ cups rich chicken stock
2 tablespoons white wine
1 small bay leaf
1 tablespoon minced celery or celery leaves
1 small piece of onion, minced
½ teaspoon salt
2 tablespoons butter
¼ cup minced fresh mushrooms
2 tablespoons flour

Pour stock into saucepan and add wine, bay leaf, celery, onion and salt. Cover and simmer for about 15 minutes. Strain. Melt butter in a clean saucepan and add mushrooms. Cook mushrooms until tender. Stir in flour and blend well. Slowly add the strained stock, stirring all the while, and cook until thick. Simmer for 5 minutes longer. Adjust seasoning if necessary. Makes about 1½ cups sauce.

# MR. AND MRS. JERRY LEWIS

# Chicken Fricassee with Dumplings

1 tender roasting chicken or capon,
    5 to 6 pounds, or 2 frying chickens,
    3 pounds each
salt and pepper
1 cup oil or shortening
½ cup liquid margarine
½ cup chopped onion
½ cup chopped green pepper
½ cup chopped fresh parsley
3 tablespoons flour
2 cups chicken stock, or more
1 cup chopped fresh mushrooms

1 tablespoon minced celery
1 teaspoon dried thyme
1 tablespoon Worcestershire sauce
3 carrots
12 tiny white onions
1 cup shelled green peas
4 ounces chopped pimientos
8 ounces sherry wine

Disjoint the chicken or chickens, as if for frying. Rub the pieces well with salt and pepper. Heat oil or shortening in a large iron skillet. When it boils, add chicken pieces, then the liquid margarine. Brown chicken pieces lightly on both sides. Remove skillet from heat, transfer chicken to a platter, and pour off about half of the liquid fat remaining in the skillet (it can be reserved for another use).

Return skillet to heat and stir in chopped onion, green pepper and parsley. Gradually add the flour, stirring constantly, and continue to cook until the ingredients melt into a warm brown. Slowly add the chicken stock (you may need more than 2 cups). Return chicken pieces to the skillet and add mushrooms, celery, thyme and Worcestershire. Cover and cook slowly for 1½ hours.

Scrape carrots and cut into 2-inch pieces. Peel onions but leave them whole. After 1½ hours, add these vegetables to the chicken. After 15 minutes, add green peas, pimientos and sherry, and simmer for 15 minutes. Serve with dumplings (recipe follows). Makes 8 servings.

68

# Dumplings

6 egg whites
3 tablespoons sugar
2 tablespoons flour
pinch of salt
4 egg yolks, beaten
2 ounces butter

Beat egg whites until stiff. Stir sugar, flour, salt and egg yolks together; mix well. Fold egg whites into this mixture. Shape dough into small dumplings and place in a baking dish. Melt the butter and pour over dumplings. Bake in a preheated 350°F. oven for 6 to 8 minutes.

These dumplings are especially good with chicken fricassee, but because they are so light and fluffy they can be used in many other ways.

# RICHARD SLATE

# Poulet d'Amour

3 green apples
3 pears
ground allspice and cinnamon
grated nutmeg
sugar
brandy and kirsch
15 small new potatoes, whole
garlic
fresh basil
1 roasting chicken, 5 pounds
oil and butter
paprika

fresh tarragon
salt and pepper
2 cups water

Wash apples and pears, cut out stem and blossom ends, and cut fruits into thick slices. Place in a bowl and sprinkle with spices and sugar to taste. Pour in liqueurs to taste and mix well. Refrigerate overnight, stirring occasionally.

Peel potatoes and place in another bowl. Add garlic, peeled and put through a press, and minced fresh basil to taste. Mix well. Refrigerate overnight, stirring occasionally.

Next day, preheat oven to 350°F. Dress and draw the chicken, fill cavity with the fruit mixture, and truss the bird. Rub chicken with a mixture of oil and butter and sprinkle with paprika, garlic, peeled and put through a press, minced fresh tarragon, and salt and pepper to taste. Arrange potatoes in the bottom of a roasting pan, and add 2 cups water. Place chicken on top, and roast in the preheated oven for 2 hours, or until tender. Baste the bird often with pan juices. Turn it on all sides for even browning. Add more water if necessary.

Serve chicken and potatoes accompanied by a salad of greens with Roquefort dressing and fresh strawberries with Champagne. Makes 6 servings.

70

# SAMMY DAVIS, JR.

# Creamed Quails

6 quails
1 onion, peeled and quartered
1 carrot, scraped and sliced
1 celery rib, trimmed and sliced
1 bay leaf
pinch of dried thyme
1 teaspoon salt
¼ teaspoon freshly ground black pepper
2 tablespoons arrowroot
¼ cup cream
¼ cup sherry wine

6 toast rounds
3 parsley sprigs, chopped

Dress and draw quails. Place them in a deep baking dish or roasting pan just large enough to hold them. Add onion, carrot, celery, bay leaf, thyme, salt and pepper. Add just enough water to cover the quails. Bring liquid to a boil, then reduce heat and simmer over low heat for 40 minutes, or until quails are tender. Bone quails and cut the meat into julienne slices.

Strain the quail broth and pour 2 cups of it into a saucepan over low heat. Stir arrowroot into the cream until dissolved, then stir the mixture into the quail broth and simmer, stirring, until it thickens to a light cream sauce. Add sherry, then mix in the julienne meat. Spoon over toast rounds and sprinkle with parsley. Makes 6 servings.

*Note:* Commercially raised quails are available by mail; however these seldom weigh more than 5 ounces, including bones. You may prefer to prepare 12 quails for 6 servings. These can be ordered from Manchester Farms, P.O. Box 97, Dalzell, South Carolina 29040.

The recipe will work just as well with Rock Cornish game birds; as these are larger, 1 bird per serving will be ample.

## JULIA MEADE

# Roast Turkey with Corn Bread Stuffing

1 turkey, 12 pounds
1 cup liquid margarine
juice of 1 lemon
salt and pepper
Corn Bread Stuffing (recipe follows)
6 tablespoons flour
milk and/or broth for gravy, if needed

Remove giblets (liver, heart, gizzard) from turkey. Cover giblets with water and bring to a simmer. Remove liver after a few minutes, long enough so it is no longer pink; save liver for stuffing. Simmer remaining giblets until tender; set both giblets and stock aside to use for gravy. Wash turkey well in cold water and pat dry with paper towels. Mix liquid margarine and lemon juice with salt and pepper to taste. Rub cavity and outside of bird well with some of this mixture; set remainder aside. Stuff bird in both cavities, but lightly to avoid a soggy, compact stuffing. Truss the bird: Fasten neck skin to the back with a skewer. Lift wings up and onto the back. Fasten abdominal opening with skewers, then lace shut with a fine cord. Tie drumsticks to tail with a cord; if there is a bridge of skin at this opening, pull drumsticks underneath the skin. Place the bird breast up on a rack in a shallow roasting pan. Again rub the entire surface with remaining margarine and lemon-juice mixture. Cover bird with a sheet of foil, pinching it at each end to keep it in place, but leaving it loose over the top and sides. Roast turkey in a preheated 325°F. oven for 4½ to 5 hours. For the last hour remove the foil so bird will become golden brown. Baste with pan drippings every 20 minutes. Remove turkey to a warm platter, remove string and skewers, and keep bird warm while making gravy.

Pour the drippings from roasting pan into a bowl, leaving the brown residue in the pan. Skim fat from drippings. Measure 6 tablespoons of the fat, and return this to roasting pan. Measure defattened turkey drippings and stock from giblets. If there is less than 4 cups, add milk or broth to reach that amount. Chop the giblets. Set roasting pan over low heat on top of the stove and stir in the flour.

**72**

Cook slowly, stirring constantly, until flour is brown. Add the 4 cups liquid and cook, still stirring, until thickened. Stir in chopped giblets and season with salt and pepper to taste. Simmer for 10 minutes. Serve in a gravy boat. Makes 12 servings.

## Corn Bread Stuffing

1 pound sausage meat
2 large onions, peeled and chopped
1 cup chopped celery
½ cup chopped mushrooms
½ cup chopped green pepper
½ cup chopped parsley
1 turkey liver, simmered briefly
1 package (12 ounces) corn bread stuffing
    mix
¼ cup white bread crumbs
2 teaspoons salt
2 teaspoons poultry seasoning
1 teaspoon dried thyme
½ teaspoon black pepper
¼ cup chicken broth
¼ cup liquid margarine

Sauté sausage meat in a heavy frying pan, breaking it apart as it cooks. Lift sausage from pan and let it drain. Pour off all but 2 tablespoons sausage drippings from the pan. Add onions, celery, mushrooms, green pepper and parsley to the drippings, and sauté until tender. Add reserved turkey liver and mash into the vegetables. Pour corn bread stuffing mix and bread crumbs into a large bowl, and add all the seasonings, the cooked sausage and sautéed vegetables. Mix well, then stir in chicken broth and liquid margarine. Makes about 10 cups stuffing, enough for a 12-pound turkey.

# MR. AND MRS. EARL WILSON

# Roast Turkey Gourmet

1 turkey, 12 pounds, dressed and ready for
    roasting
½ tablespoon mixed ground ginger and
    grated nutmeg
salt and pepper
paprika
Mrs. Wilson's Dressing (recipe follows)
¾ cup liquid margarine
½ cup white wine
8 ounces frozen orange-juice concentrate
flour
½ cup boiling water
parsley

12 canned pear halves
12 canned peach halves
24 sugar cubes
1 tablespoon lemon extract
1 tablespoon brandy

Rub the turkey inside and out with a mixture of the ginger and nutmeg and salt, pepper and paprika to taste. Stuff the bird with Mrs. Wilson's dressing. Mix margarine, wine and orange-juice concentrate, and rub all over the outside of the bird. Sprinkle bird lightly with flour. Roast in a preheated 325°F. oven for 30 minutes. Pour the boiling water into the roasting pan, and roast for about 5 hours longer, basting every 20 minutes with the pan drippings. To ensure an evenly browned bird, place it first on one side; when brown, turn to the other side; finally, place bird on its back for remainder of roasting time. When turkey is done, transfer it to a large platter or tray covered with parsley.

Drain pear and peach halves thoroughly, and arrange them alternately around the bird. Dip 12 sugar cubes into lemon extract and place each one in the hollow of a pear half. Dip remaining 12 sugar cubes into brandy and place each one in the hollow of a peach half. When ready to serve, ignite the sugar cubes and present the bird surrounded by the flaming garnish. Makes 12 servings.

74

# Mrs. Wilson's Dressing

1 large green pepper
1 medium-size onion
3 large celery ribs
1 tablespoon chicken fat
1 tablespoon shortening
1 large loaf of day-old bread
ground sage
salt and pepper

Trim pepper, remove ribs and seeds, and dice. Peel and slice onion. Wash and trim celery and cut into ⅛-inch pieces. Sauté vegetables in the mixed fat and shortening for about 10 minutes, until onion is translucent. Shred bread, moisten with water, then drain in a colander to let excess water run out. Add bread to vegetables and mix. Season with sage, salt and pepper to taste. Stuff turkey.

To bake stuffing outside the bird, arrange in the roaster around the turkey, about 45 minutes before the bird is done. Baste stuffing with pan juices. It will be ready when turkey is done.

# THE HONORABLE
# FRITZ W. ALEXANDER II

# Roast Stuffed Goose

1 goose, 9 pounds
salt and freshly ground pepper
½ teaspoon dried thyme
½ teaspoon dried marjoram
½ lemon
Corn Bread Stuffing (recipe follows)
3 cups chicken stock, or more
1 cup water
1 cup sliced celery, or more
1 onion, peeled and sliced
2 tablespoons flour

Remove large pieces of fat from cavity of goose, and rub the outside well with the fat. Sprinkle salt and pepper into the cavity. Mix thyme and marjoram with more salt and pepper and rub this mixture all over the outside of the bird. Rub goose with the lemon half, squeezing the juice over the bird. Set goose aside, and prepare the stuffing.

Preheat oven to 400°F. Fill cavity with stuffing, and close with skewers. Truss goose with string so that wings and drumsticks are tied close to the body. Pour chicken stock and water into the roasting pan, and make a bed with celery and onion slices (use more if needed). Place goose on the vegetable bed and roast in the preheated oven for 1 hour, basting every 15 minutes. Reduce heat to 300°F., and add more stock and water to the pan if needed. After 2½ hours test the drumstick; it should move easily in the socket if the bird is done. If you pierce the flesh with a skewer, the juices should be clear.

Remove goose to a warm platter. Pour off the pan liquid, and skim off the fat. Add flour to the pan, stir into the drippings, and brown flour over medium heat on top of the stove. Stir in the pan liquid, or add more stock if needed, and stir until smooth. Reduce sauce over high heat to the desired consistency. Season well, and strain into a gravy boat. Makes 8 servings.

# Corn Bread Stuffing

1 tablespoon butter
2 tablespoons oil
1 cup chopped onion
1 cup chopped celery
2 tablespoons chicken stock
1 package (6 ounces) dressing mix
1 package (15 ounces) corn bread mix
1 teaspoon salt
1 teaspoon ground sage
¼ teaspoon black pepper
¼ teaspoon dried thyme
4 eggs
1 cup milk
3 tablespoons Cognac

Heat butter and oil in a skillet, and in it sauté onion and celery until onion is beginning to brown on the edges. Add the stock and remove from heat. In a large bowl combine dressing mix, corn bread mix and all seasonings. Beat 3 eggs lightly and add to dry ingredients. Beat the last egg with the milk and add to the bowl. Finally add Cognac, mix well, then scrape the sautéed mixture from the skillet into the bowl, and mix everything together. Makes about 8 cups stuffing, enough for an 8-pound goose.

   If you like, cooked peeled chestnuts, oysters or sausages can be added to the stuffing.

# Duckling with Black Cherry Sauce

1 Long Island duckling, 5 pounds
½ tablespoon salt
2 teaspoons paprika
2 teaspoons poultry seasoning
1 teaspoon pepper
½ cup port wine
1 whole clove
pinch of ground allspice
pinch of grated nutmeg
pinch of dried thyme
1 teaspoon grated orange rind
½ cup bottled brown sauce
½ cup currant jelly
½ cup pitted black cherries
juice of ½ orange
1 tablespoon butter

Cut duckling into quarters. Mix salt, paprika, poultry seasoning and pepper, and rub the mixture into the duckling pieces. Place duckling, skin side down, in a dry skillet—an electric skillet set at 350°F. or a large skillet placed over medium heat on a gas or electric stove. Cover skillet tightly and cook, turning at 20-minute intervals, until duck pieces are uniformly browned and cooked through. When this step is completed, pour off the fat.

Add wine, spices, thyme and orange rind to duck pieces, and simmer over moderate heat until the liquid is reduced to half. Add brown sauce and blend well with reduced wine. Add jelly and heat until dissolved. Add black cherries, orange juice and butter, and heat until sauce is simmering. Makes 4 servings.

# JOHNNY MATHIS

# Wild Duck
# à la Mathis

*Choose ducks that have been fed only on grain or rice. "They are not as fishy tasting," says Johnny.*

2 or 3 wild ducks
salt and pepper
½ cup chopped onion
1 green pepper, sliced
2 or 3 celery ribs, sliced
3 cups water

Clean ducks. Rub with salt and pepper. Place ducks, breast side up, in a roasting pan. Add onion, green pepper slices, celery and water to pan. Cover, and bake in a preheated 325°F. oven for 2 hours, or until ducks are tender. Baste occasionally with pan juices during roasting. Serve on a bed of wild rice. Makes 4 to 6 servings.

# LADY VIOLET BRADDON

# Pheasant with Apples

2 medium-size pheasants, dressed
¼ pound butter (1 stick)
2 large tart apples
4 ounces apple brandy
   (applejack or Calvados)
1½ cups heavy cream
juice of 1 lemon
salt and pepper

Truss pheasants: tie wings close to the body and tie legs together. Melt butter in a large heavy skillet, and cook birds in it until browned on all sides. Remove birds to a platter and keep warm. Peel and core apples and cut into slices. Sauté slices in the skillet used for the birds until they are slightly browned. Transfer apples to a 3-quart casserole or roasting pan. Put pheasants on top. Add apple brandy. Bake in a preheated 375°F. oven for 45 minutes. Remove casserole from oven and pour in cream and lemon juice. Add salt and pepper to taste. Cover casserole and return to oven. Cook for 1 hour longer, until pheasants are tender. Makes 8 servings.

# PRINCESS
MONIQUE SIHANOUK

# Sautéed Doves

24 doves, dressed and drawn (see Note)
salt and pepper
½ pound butter (2 sticks)
12 tablespoons Worcestershire sauce
12 slices of bacon, halved
1 garlic clove, peeled
3 bay leaves
½ cup flour
1½ cups chicken bouillon
2 lemons
2 oranges
12 ounces sherry wine

Rinse doves, pat dry, and sprinkle each one with salt and pepper. Melt the butter, a part at a time, in a large heavy skillet, and brown doves, a few at a time, in the butter. Split each dove down the back and remove the backbone. Pull sides together so each bird still looks whole, and place them, breast sides down, in a large shallow baking dish or roasting pan that will hold them all in a single layer. Sprinkle each dove with ½ tablespoon Worcestershire sauce and lay a half-slice of bacon on each bird. Put garlic in the bottom of the pan and place the bay leaves among the birds. Sprinkle doves with flour, and pour chicken bouillon into the bottom of the pan. Bake in a preheated 450°F. oven for 30 minutes.

Carefully pour off all the liquid from the baking dish and skim off the fat. Let the liquid stand for 30 minutes. Cut each lemon and each orange into 12 slices; discard end pieces, and remove any pits. Arrange lemon and orange slices around the birds. Strain the reserved pan liquid over the doves. Bake doves in a 300°F. oven for 30 minutes. Carefully remove bacon pieces, and pour 1 tablespoon sherry over each bird. Return dish to oven and bake for 30 minutes longer, or until doves are tender. Serve with wild rice and spiced red apple rings. Makes 12 servings.

*Note:* This recipe calls for doves, which are wild birds, hence not used for food in the United States. Instead, use 12 squabs, about 1 pound each, or 24 commercially raised quails, 5 to 6 ounces each.

# 6

## MEATS

CARL STOKES

# Savory Roast Beef

1 standing 3-rib beef roast,
    about 9 pounds,
    ready for roasting
¼ teaspoon dried marjoram
¼ teaspoon dried thyme
¼ teaspoon dried savory
¼ teaspoon dried basil
½ teaspoon salt
⅛ teaspoon pepper
1 teaspoon meat extract
½ cup hot water
1½ cups red Burgundy wine
6 tablespoons all-purpose flour
1¼ cups water

Preheat oven to 325°F. Place beef, fat side up, in a shallow roasting pan; do not use a rack but let the beef rest on its bones. Mix well the herbs, salt and pepper, and rub the mixture into the surface of the beef on all sides. Insert a meat thermometer through outside fat into thickest part of muscle; the point of the thermometer should not rest on fat or bone. Dissolve meat extract in ½ cup hot water; add ½ cup of the wine. Use some of the liquid to baste the beef. Roast the beef uncovered, basting it several times with remaining liquid mixture. Roast until thermometer registers 140°F. for rare, 3¼ to 3¾ hours; or 160°F. for medium, 3¾ to 4¼ hours; or 170°F. for well done, 4¼ to 4¾ hours.

Remove roast to a heated platter and let it stand in a warm place for 20 minutes before carving. Meanwhile make gravy. Pour off drippings from roasting pan into a measuring cup. Return 6 tablespoons of the drippings to the roaster and stir in the flour to make a smooth mixture. Gradually add 1¼ cups water and remaining wine, stirring until all brown bits in the roaster are dissolved and gravy is smooth. Makes about 12 servings.

# JANE COOKE WRIGHT, M.D.

# Party Roast Beef with Onion Pie

1 boned 14-pound beef roast,
    loin strip or prime ribs
4 garlic cloves, peeled and split
8 bay leaves
½ cup lemon juice
½ cup Worcestershire sauce
3 tablespoons finely crushed black
    peppercorns
salt

Preheat oven to 350°F. Rub beef all over with cut side of garlic cloves. Place beef in a roasting pan and arrange bay leaves around it. Sprinkle with lemon juice and Worcestershire, and scatter crushed pepper all over. Roast for 20 minutes per pound. About 30 minutes before serving, sprinkle with salt. Slice beef thin and serve hot with onion pie (recipe follows). Makes 14 to 20 servings.

## Onion Pie

pastry for 1-crust, 9-inch pie
2 cups chopped onions
2 tablespoons vegetable oil
1 teaspoon salt
2 cups dairy sour cream
4 eggs
¼ cup chopped fresh parsley
paprika
crumbled crisp bacon (optional)

Preheat oven to 400°F. Roll out pastry to a sheet large enough to line an 8- or 9-inch square baking pan with removable bottom. Fit pastry into the pan, line with foil and pie weights, and bake for 10 minutes. Remove weights and foil and bake for 10 minutes longer, until partially baked. Cool. Reduce oven heat to 350°F.

Cook onions in oil until soft but not browned. Add salt. Remove from heat and cool. Beat sour cream and eggs together until smooth. Add to cooled onions, mix well, then spoon into the pie shell. Bake for 1 hour, or until the pie is golden brown. Sprinkle parsley and paprika on top. Add crumbled bacon if your guests like the flavor. Cut into small squares and serve around the roast beef. Makes about 16 squares, about 2-inch size.

ARNOLD SCHWARZENEGGER

# Roast Marinated Beef

1 boneless beef roast, 6 pounds
1 cup wine vinegar
1 cup dry red Bordeaux wine
½ cup salad oil
2 onions, peeled and sliced
1 celery rib, chopped
1 teaspoon salt

4 peppercorns
2 bay leaves
2 whole cloves
2 tablespoons brown bouquet sauce
2 cups fresh beef bouillon
2 to 3 pounds prepared fresh vegetables
    (your choice)

Place beef in an earthenware, glass or ceramic bowl. Make a marinade of next 9 ingredients and pour it over beef. If possible, marinade should cover the meat; if it does not, turn the beef in the marinade several times. Refrigerate overnight.

    Remove beef from marinade, wipe dry, and brush with brown bouquet sauce. Roast in a preheated 350°F. oven for 1½ to 2 hours. Add bouillon and vegetables and roast for 1 hour longer. Makes 8 servings.

# MADAME DE CONGE (BRICKTOP)

# Italian Pot Roast with Noodles

3 pounds boneless beef chuck or rump
2 tablespoons vegetable oil
2 garlic cloves
2 medium-size onions, chopped
½ tablespoon dried orégano
1 teaspoon dried thyme
½ teaspoon dried basil
⅛ teaspoon ground cinnamon
1 teaspoon salt
¼ teaspoon black pepper
½ teaspoon sugar
12 ounces tomato paste
3 cups water

1 pound thin noodles
grated Parmesan cheese (optional)
snipped fresh chives (optional)

Wipe meat with a damp cloth and dry well. Heat oil in a heavy saucepan, and brown meat in it on all sides. Remove meat, and reduce heat. Peel garlic and push through a press into the oil. Add onions, herbs, salt, pepper and sugar. Simmer for about 5 minutes, being careful not to burn the seasonings. Return meat to the pan. Mix tomato paste with water and pour over meat. Bring to a boil, reduce heat, and cover loosely. Simmer slowly, turning the meat occasionally, for 2 to 3 hours.

When meat is tender, cook noodles and drain. Slice the roast and arrange slices on a bed of noodles. Cover with sauce from pot-roasting. Sprinkle with cheese and chives if desired. Makes 6 servings.

# MRS. RONALD REAGAN

# Elegant Flaming Beef

*"A filet of beef can be the most succulent meat in the world. I serve this dish so it looks like a real production, on a large silver tea tray with the edges covered with parsley. The meat platter is centered on the tray, with a silver sauceboat and a smaller tray for the block of pâté. A tenderloin is easy to carve, but be sure to carve thin slices as a base for the pâté and sauce,"* says Mrs. Reagan.

1 piece of beef filet (tenderloin),
    about 4 pounds
4 ounces Sercial (dry) Madeira wine
cracked black peppercorns

⅓ cup melted butter
1 can (7½ ounces) pâté de foie gras
8 ounces brandy
Truffled Madeira Sauce (recipe follows)

Have the beef cut from the large end of the filet; it should be about 10 inches long and well trimmed. Wipe meat well with a wet paper towel, and set it in a roasting pan. Pour half of the Madeira (¼ cup) over the meat. Sprinkle liberally with cracked black peppercorns. Put in a cold oven and turn the control to 300°F. Make a basting sauce with the melted butter and remaining Madeira, and keep it hot. Roast the filet for 1½ hours, basting 4 times at even intervals, first with some of the basting sauce. Next time, remove pan from oven and pour drippings into the basting sauce; baste again. After the first 30 minutes, turn beef over to brown the underside. Third time, skim any fat from the pan drippings before pouring it into the basting sauce; baste again, and again for the fourth time.

While beef cooks, slice the pâté. Refrigerate pâté, and cut with a hot knife into the thinnest possible slices. Lay slices overlapping on the serving tray, and slide tray and all into a plastic bag. Refrigerate until time to serve.

Slice a portion off the base of the meat so it will be level, and place on a warmed heatproof platter. Pour the sauce from the roasting pan over the meat. When guests are assembled, pour the brandy over and ignite it. Keep spooning the sauce and brandy over the meat until flames die out; the burning brandy blends all the flavors. Carve the beef; top each slice with a slice of the pâté and a spoonful of the truffled Madeira sauce. Each piece of filet will have medium, well-done and rare meat; the ends are more done than the center. Makes 6 servings.

## Truffled Madeira Sauce

2 very large truffles, chopped
8 mushroom stems, chopped
⅓ cup Madeira wine
1 can (10½ ounces) condensed beef
    bouillon
2 teaspoons arrowroot

Marinate truffles and mushroom stems in the Madeira. Pour 3 tablespoons bouillon into a cup and dissolve the arrowroot in it. Heat the balance of the bouillon, undiluted, and stir in the dissolved arrowroot. Cook over very low heat, stirring, for about 5 minutes. Add truffles, mushrooms and Madeira, and heat, stirring gently, for 1 to 2 minutes. Make the sauce a day ahead and store, covered, in the refrigerator. Heat sauce to serve. Makes about 1¼ cups.

# SYD SIMONS

# Syd's Oriental Steak

5 pounds sirloin steak, 2¼ inches thick
½ cup soy sauce
½ cup brown sugar
3 tablespoons oil
3 tablespoons honey
1 teaspoon garlic powder
1 teaspoon ground ginger
½ cup chopped green onions (scallions)

Remove bone and fat from steak, and cut meat into slices ½ inch thick. Combine remaining ingredients to make a marinade, and marinate steak slices in it, in a glass or ceramic container, for 1 hour. Turn the slices occasionally.

For rare steak, broil slices over a hot charcoal fire for 2 minutes on each side. Transfer from grill to a heated platter or individual plates. Spoon a little warm marinade over steak, and serve. If you like your steak very rare, cook for only 30 seconds on each side. Makes 4 to 6 servings.

# LIZ SMITH

# Texas Chicken-Fried Steak

Buy ½ pound round steak per person, and ask your butcher to cut it into ⅛-inch-thick slices, "sliced thin for frying." Lay the slices on a flat surface and sprinkle with black pepper. Beat slices on both sides with a mallet or heavy bottle to tenderize them. Trim off any fat, and cut slices into small pieces like the scallops for veal piccata.

Beat eggs in a shallow bowl. Dump flour on a flat plate. Heat vegetable oil in a frying pan until fairly hot. Dip beef pieces into egg, then into flour, then place in hot oil and fry fairly fast. Turn over to brown the other side, and remove to paper towels. Sprinkle with salt only *after* frying.

Make gravy: Pour off excess fat from frying pan, but leave as much of the meat drippings as possible. Put over moderate heat and add 1 or 2 teaspoons flour. Stir flour into drippings to thicken gravy. Add a mixture of milk and water; you can use whole milk, skim milk, or half and half, depending on how rich you want the gravy to be. The taste will be the same, whatever you use. Keep stirring the mixture, and taste it; add salt and pepper. If gravy becomes too thick, add more milk or water. If it is not thick enough, stir in instant flour, a little at a time, until it thickens. Pour gravy into a pitcher or sauceboat and set it over a candle warmer to keep hot.

Serve with biscuits, potatoes, and a salad of lettuce and tomatoes, or pineapple chunks, or lettuce with Cheddar cheese bits and mayonnaise. Steaks are good hot or cold. You can drink anything with this: soft drinks, beer, Champagne, or very good white or red French wine.

# NAOMI SIMS

# Steak and Kidney Pie

pastry for 2-crust, 9-inch deep-dish pie
1 porterhouse steak
2 beef kidneys
2 medium-size onions
5 large fresh mushrooms
4 ounces butter
2 cups boiling water
2 tablespoons Worcestershire sauce
1 teaspoon salt
1 teaspoon pepper
1 teaspoon ground cinnamon
½ teaspoon ground ginger
3 tablespoons dry red wine

*Naomi Sims says, "I always bake two at a time and freeze one for later; just pop it into the oven at 450°F. and bake for 45 minutes."*

Make pastry, roll out into 2 rounds, and use one to line a deep-dish pie pan. Trim steak and kidneys; save the fat. Cut steak into 1-inch cubes, kidneys into ½-inch cubes. Peel and slice onions. Trim and chop mushrooms. Melt fat from steak and kidneys in a large skillet. Add onions and mushrooms and sauté until onions are brown. Add butter, steak and kidneys. Cook until meat is brown on both sides, then add boiling water, Worcestershire, salt, pepper, cinnamon and ginger. Stir, then turn heat to low, cover, and simmer for 60 to 90 minutes, until meat is very tender. Add small amounts of water from time to time as needed; do not let the meat get dry.

Preheat oven to 450°F. When meat is cooked, add the wine and turn everything into the pastry-lined pan. Roll the top crust over, crimp to the lower crust, and make a few holes for steam to escape. Bake in the preheated oven for about 30 minutes, until the crust is golden brown. Serve hot with fresh peas and carrots, coleslaw, and a chilled white wine. Makes 6 servings.

# DIAHANN CARROLL

# Brown Beef Stew

2 pounds boneless beef chuck
2 tablespoons fat
4 cups boiling water
10 ½ ounces condensed clear beef
    consommé
1 teaspoon lemon juice
1 medium-size onion, peeled and sliced
1 garlic clove, peeled
2 bay leaves
1 beef bouillon cube
1 tablespoon salt
1 teaspoon sugar
1 teaspoon Worcestershire sauce
½ teaspoon black pepper
½ teaspoon paprika
dash of ground allspice or cloves

1 ½ cups dry red wine
6 carrots, scraped and quartered
1 pound small white onions, peeled but
    whole
6 potatoes, peeled and cubed (optional)
flour (optional)

Have beef cut into 1½-inch cubes. Sauté them in the fat in a large heavy kettle, until cubes are well browned on all sides. Add boiling water, consommé, lemon juice, sliced onion, garlic, bay leaves, bouillon cube and seasonings. Bring liquid to a boil, then reduce heat and simmer for 2 hours, stirring occasionally to prevent sticking. Add wine, carrots, onions, and potatoes if you use them. Continue simmering for 20 to 30 minutes, or until all vegetables are done. Transfer meat and vegetables to a large serving bowl. Discard bay leaves. Thicken liquid with flour for gravy if you like. Makes 8 servings.

# BEVERLY SILLS

# Sukiyaki

2 tablespoons chopped beef suet
3 cups thin-sliced onions
1 bunch of green onions (scallions),
    chopped fine
1 whole celery stalk, washed and sliced
5 ounces canned bamboo shoots,
    drained
5 ounces canned water chestnuts, drained
2 cups bean sprouts
⅓ cup blanched almonds
1 pound fresh spinach, washed and drained
1 cup sliced fresh mushrooms
2 pounds beef for London broil
    (top round or flank), cut into
    ⅛-inch-thick slices
⅓ cup sugar
⅓ cup tomato juice
⅓ cup Worcestershire sauce

2 tablespoons soy sauce
1 pound bean curd, cubed or sliced
¾ cup chicken stock or canned
    chicken broth

Make this dish over a hibachi, outdoors in summer, or in an indoor fireplace or on a well-insulated card table in winter. Coat a Chinese wok with the suet, and heat. Stir in onions, scallions, celery, bamboo shoots, water chestnuts, bean sprouts, almonds and spinach. Cook, stirring, for 5 minutes. Add mushrooms and cook and stir for another 5 minutes. Add sliced beef, the sugar, tomato juice, Worcestershire, soy sauce and bean curd. Stir and cook for 15 minutes longer. Stir in chicken stock and cook for 8 to 10 minutes. Serve with rice. Makes 8 servings.

LIV ULLMAN

# Norjapcan Foo Young and Vegetables

10 dried black mushrooms
4 pounds boneless beef
2 tablespoons oil
1 onion, peeled and chopped
1 teaspoon minced garlic
10 water chestnuts, diced
1 teaspoon minced fresh gingerroot
1 teaspoon black pepper
salt
1 cup water or dry saké
1 cup mirin

1 tablespoon cornstarch
1 cup Japanese soy sauce
1 pound fresh snow peas, trimmed
1 green pepper, cut into slivers
4 green onions (scallions), sliced
8 thin slices of carrot
8 slices of bamboo shoot
grated rind of 1 orange
2 cups Japanese noodles (kishimen),
    cooked

Place dried mushrooms in a bowl and cover with hot water. Let stand for 30 minutes or longer to soften. Drain mushrooms and squeeze dry. Chop them, or cut into small slices. Cut the beef into thin slices. Heat the oil in a large skillet or top-of-the-stove casserole. Brown the beef slices in oil, turning to brown all sides. Add onion, garlic, mushrooms, water chestnuts, ginger, black pepper, and salt to taste. Cover the pan and cook for 30 minutes. Add water and *mirin,* and continue to cook over low heat until beef is tender.

Stir cornstarch into soy sauce, and stir into the beef mixture. Add the vegetables and cook for 10 minutes. Sprinkle orange rind over all, and serve over the cooked noodles. Makes 8 servings.

*Note*: If you cannot find saké (rice wine), use a dry white wine. If you cannot find *mirin,* which is a sweet saké, use a medium-sweet sherry. If you cannot find Japanese noodles, use Italian linguine or fettuccine, or broad egg noodles.

THE HONORABLE ROBERT O. LOWERY

# Oxtail à la Catalane

5 pounds oxtails
½ cup flour
2 teaspoons salt
1 teaspoon freshly ground black pepper
2 ounces butter
½ cup dry red wine
2 tomatoes, peeled and chopped
2 large onions, peeled and chopped
2 garlic cloves, peeled and minced
5 medium-size carrots, scraped and
    quartered
1 medium-size white turnip, peeled and
    quartered

1 cup chopped green pepper
2 bay leaves
½ teaspoon dried orégano
½ teaspoon cayenne pepper
2 cans (10½ ounces each) clear consommé
1 cup water
1 cup dry Madeira wine
12 new potatoes, peeled
12 scallions, chopped
1 cup cooked green peas
2 tablespoons chopped fresh parsley

Wash and dry oxtails and cut them into 2-inch pieces. Mix flour with salt and pepper, and shake oxtail pieces in the flour until well coated. Melt butter in a large heavy pot and brown oxtails. Remove oxtails from pot and pour off the fat.

Add red wine to the pan and stir over low heat for 2 minutes to deglaze the pan. Return oxtails to the pot and add tomatoes, onions and garlic, 2 carrots, the turnip, green pepper, bay leaves, orégano and cayenne. Pour in consommé and water. Bring liquid to a boil, reduce to a simmer, cover the pot, and simmer for 3 hours. Cool the stew. Remove and discard carrot and turnip pieces and the bay leaves. Refrigerate the stew overnight.

About 1½ hours before serving, remove stew from refrigerator and lift off the layer of fat that has risen to the top. Bring stew slowly to a boil, reduce to a simmer, and gently stir in the Madeira. Taste for seasoning and add more salt and pepper if needed. Add whole potatoes, remaining carrot quarters and the scallions, and simmer slowly for 45 minutes, or until vegetables are tender. Gently stir in cooked peas and parsley. Place the oxtails in the center of a large platter and arrange the vegetables around. Makes 12 servings.

# PRESIDENT DWIGHT D. EISENHOWER

# Meat Loaf

6 slices of white bread
3 cups milk
1 pound lean pork
1 pound beef
½ cup heavy cream
1 egg, slightly beaten
2 teaspoons salt
1 teaspoon freshly ground black pepper
4 hard-cooked eggs
7 or 8 strips of bacon

8 new potatoes, scrubbed
1 cup consommé

Soak the bread in the milk, then squeeze bread until it is fairly dry. The mixture of half lean pork and half beef will give better texture. Grind both meats once through a food grinder, then grind a second time with the soaked bread. Turn into a bowl and add cream, beaten egg, salt and pepper. Mix well. Shell the hard-cooked eggs.

Roll or mold the meat loaf rather than packing it in a loaf pan. Use a baking dish large enough so the meat will not touch the sides. Lay 3 or 4 strips of bacon down the center of the baking dish. Form the loaf on a double sheet of wax paper so it will be easy to slide it into the pan. Put half of the meat mixture on the paper and shape into the bottom half of the meat loaf. Lay the shelled eggs in a straight line down the middle. Place remaining meat mixture on top and shape into the top half of the loaf, completely enclosing the eggs. Slide loaf on top of bacon strips, then lay remaining 4 bacon strips on top (for flavor). Arrange potatoes around the loaf. Bake in a preheated 375°F. oven, basting as necessary with the consommé, for 1½ hours. Makes 8 servings.

## PEARL BAILEY

# Burgundy Meatballs

2 pounds boneless beef chuck, ground
1 cup fresh bread crumbs
1 large onion, peeled and grated
1 garlic clove, peeled and minced
1 teaspoon dried orégano
½ teaspoon dried rosemary
¼ teaspoon dried thyme
½ cup milk
1 tablespoon dry mustard
1 tablespoon Worcestershire sauce
1 teaspoon Tabasco
5 slices of bacon
flour
2 tablespoons oil
1¼ cups water
1 cup red Burgundy wine
1 teaspoon salt
1 teaspoon brown sugar

Put ground chuck in a large bowl and add bread crumbs, onion, garlic, herbs, milk, mustard, Worcestershire and Tabasco. Mix all together with a fork. In a large skillet cook the bacon until crisp. Remove from pan, dry on paper towels, and crumble. Add bacon to the beef and again mix. Shape meat into round balls. Stir 2 tablespoons flour into the bacon drippings and set the skillet aside.

Heat oil in another skillet. Roll meatballs in flour and cook in the oil until browned on all sides. Pour off the oil. Pour water and wine into the bacon dripping and flour mixture in the first skillet, and stir in salt and brown sugar. Cook over low heat until sauce is slightly thickened, about 10 minutes. Add meatballs, and simmer over very low heat for 30 minutes. Serve meatballs and sauce over rice. Makes 8 servings.

## ARNOLD AND WINNIE PALMER

# Hawaiian Meatballs with Sweet-Sour Sauce

1 ½ pounds ground beef
⅔ cup cracker crumbs
⅔ cup evaporated milk
½ cup chopped onion

1 teaspoon seasoned salt
⅓ cup flour
3 tablespoons shortening
Sweet-Sour Sauce (recipe follows)

Combine beef with cracker crumbs, evaporated milk, onion and seasoned salt; mix lightly but thoroughly. Shape mixture into 30 balls. Roll in flour, then brown in hot shortening. Pour off excess fat, and spoon sauce over meatballs. Simmer, covered, for 15 minutes. Makes 6 servings.

## Sweet-Sour Sauce

1 can (13 ½ ounces) pineapple chunks
2 tablespoons cornstarch
½ cup vinegar
½ cup brown sugar
2 tablespoons soy sauce
2 tablespoons lemon juice
1 cup coarsely chopped green pepper
1 tablespoon chopped pimiento

Drain syrup from pineapple into a measuring cup and add enough water to make 1 cup. Reserve pineapple chunks. Stir cornstarch into pineapple liquid until smooth. Stir in vinegar, brown sugar, soy sauce and lemon juice. Cook over low heat until sauce is thickened and clear. Add pineapple chunks, green pepper and pimiento; mix well. Cover, and simmer over low heat for 15 minutes. Makes about 4 cups.

TOM SNYDER

# Heavenly Hamburger

5 pounds beef chuck or round
5 pounds boneless cooked turkey
2 large green peppers
2 large onions
5 garlic cloves
1 cup chopped parsley
1 can (10½ ounces) chicken noodle soup
4 tablespoons Worcestershire sauce
4 tablespoons dry mustard
2 tablespoons seasoned salt˚
1 tablespoon black pepper
1 teaspoon cuminseeds
8 eggs, lightly beaten
2 cups cracker crumbs

Have beef and turkey ground thoroughly, then mix well together. Wash and trim peppers, discard ribs and seeds, and chop. Peel and chop onions. Peel and mince garlic. Drop all these vegetables and the parsley into a blender container and add soup, Worcestershire, all the seasonings and the eggs. Blend well. (If your blender is not large enough to hold it all, do it part at a time, then combine in a large bowl.) Mix well with the beef and turkey. Slowly add cracker crumbs until mixture is firm enough so that you can form a single hamburger. Shape the whole mixture into hamburgers, wrap them individually in wax paper, then in freezer bags, and store in the freezer for future use. Makes at least 40 hamburgers.

Serve with a cheese of your choice which is a good partner to hamburgers.

# MRS. BENNETTA WASHINGTON

# Edna's Beef Cacciatora

2½ pounds cooked tender roast beef
½ cup olive oil
2 garlic cloves, peeled and sliced thin
3½ cups sieved canned tomatoes
1¼ teaspoons salt
1 teaspoon dried orégano
1 teaspoon minced fresh parsley
½ teaspoon black pepper
1 pound fresh mushrooms
1 small onion
3 tablespoons butter

Cut beef into cubes. Heat oil in a large skillet and add garlic slices and beef. Sauté, turning beef pieces often, until browned. Add tomatoes, salt, orégano, parsley and pepper, and cook over low heat for about 25 minutes.

While beef cooks, wash mushrooms, roll in a towel to dry, and trim the stems. Slice mushrooms. Peel and mince onion. Sauté both in the butter until delicately browned. Add to beef, mix well, and simmer for 10 to 15 minutes longer. Serve with spaghetti or noodles. Makes about 6 servings.

102

# THE HONORABLE
## MRS. ERSA H. POSTON

# Poston's Pre-Payday Casserole

2 tablespoons butter or oil
½ cup minced onion
½ cup minced green pepper
¾ pound beef chuck or round, chopped
2 cups tomato sauce
¾ cup water
salt and pepper
butter or oil for casserole
1 cup uncooked rice
1 can (12 ounces) whole kernel corn

4 strips of bacon
New York State sharp cheese, grated

Preheat oven to 350°F. Heat butter or oil in a large heavy skillet. Sauté onion and green pepper until onion is translucent. Add chopped beef and brown; break up meat with a fork if it tends to clump together. Add 1 cup of the tomato sauce and ¼ cup water. Season with salt and pepper to taste. Simmer for 15 minutes.

Butter or oil a 2-quart casserole and pour rice into the bottom. Add the corn, remaining cup of tomato sauce and ½ cup water. Spoon the meat mixture into the middle. Place bacon strips across the top, or sprinkle with some of the cheese. Cover the casserole and bake in the preheated oven for 45 minutes. Uncover, sprinkle top with cheese, and return to oven to bake until cheese is browned. Makes 6 servings.

MARIO MORENO (CANTINFLAS)

# Cantinflas Tamale Pie

4 cups cold water
1 cup cornmeal
1 teaspoon salt
butter for pan
2 tablespoons bacon fat
1 cup chopped onions
2 garlic cloves, peeled and minced
1 pound ground beef
½ cup chopped celery

1 green pepper, trimmed and chopped
2 cups canned tomatoes
2 tablespoons ketchup
4 dashes of Tabasco
1 teaspoon salt
½ teaspoon dried orégano
½ cup raisins, chopped
2 pimientos, chopped
½ cup stuffed green olives

In a large saucepan bring 3 cups of the water to a boil. In a bowl mix the cornmeal and salt into remaining cup of cold water. Pour this into the boiling water, stirring constantly, and cook until cornmeal thickens. Butter a deep 12-inch pie plate with a high rim, and line it with half of the cornmeal mush.

Preheat oven to 350°F. Heat bacon fat in a large skillet, and in it sauté onions and garlic until golden. Add beef, stirring constantly. Mix vegetables, ketchup, Tabasco, salt and orégano, and stir into the beef. Cook together for 30 minutes. Add chopped raisins and pimientos at the last. Spoon half of the beef mixture into the cornmeal shell, then with a slotted spoon add the rest of the beef mixture. Cover with the rest of the mush. Set the pie plate on a large baking sheet (to protect oven, as the filling may bubble up and boil over). Bake in the preheated oven for 1½ hours. Cut into squares to serve, and garnish with the stuffed olives. Makes 8 servings.

104

# LUCILLE BALL

# Lucy's Big Gang Special

3 Bermuda onions
2 large green peppers
1 garlic clove
3 tablespoons vegetable oil
4 pounds beef round, ground
2 cans (35 ounces each) solid-pack tomatoes
1 pound egg noodles
salt and pepper

Peel and dice onions. Wash and trim peppers, remove ribs and seeds, and dice peppers. Peel and mince garlic, or put through a press. Heat the oil in a large heavy saucepan or top-of-the-stove casserole, and in it sauté the vegetables until onions are translucent. Add ground beef and cook, turning it in the pan to brown it all. Add tomatoes and the juice from the cans. Simmer over low heat, stirring occasionally, for 45 minutes.

While meat cooks, bring a large pot of water to a boil, add 2 tablespoons salt, and drop in the noodles. Cook noodles until just done; they must not be mushy as they will be cooked further. Drain well. When beef has cooked for 45 minutes, turn drained noodles into the saucepan or casserole and mix gently. Simmer for 15 minutes longer. Season with salt and pepper to taste. Makes 8 servings, or more.

# CHRISTIAAN BARNARD, M.D.

# Veal Scaloppini with Tomatoes

1 ½ pounds boneless veal,
      cut into scallops
flour
1 tablespoon butter
1 tablespoon olive oil
½ pound mushrooms, cut into thin slices
1 small garlic clove, peeled
2 tablespoons chopped fresh parsley
2 tablespoons chopped fresh basil
½ cup chopped fresh tomatoes,
      without peels or seeds
½ cup dry Marsala wine
2 tablespoons grated Parmesan cheese

Preheat oven to 325°F. Pound the scallops flat, and cut into 1-inch squares. Sprinkle with flour. Heat butter and oil in a shallow baking dish on top of the stove and brown the veal squares on both sides. Add mushrooms and push garlic through a press into the dish. Add parsley, basil, tomatoes and wine, and gently mix together. Sprinkle cheese over all. Bake in the preheated oven for 45 minutes. Makes 3 or 4 servings.

## MR. AND MRS. ROBERT GOULET

# Veal Scaloppini with Peppers

1 ½ pounds veal scallops
2 tablespoons vegetable oil
1 cup thin slices of onion
1 cup thin slices of green pepper
flour
1 cup dry Marsala wine, or more
1 cup chicken broth
2 ounces Parmesan cheese, grated

Pound scallops flat. Heat vegetable oil in a large skillet and sauté onion and green-pepper slices until lightly browned. With a skimmer lift the vegetables to a plate and keep warm. Dip veal scallops into flour, shake off excess, then sauté in the oil and vegetable juices remaining in the skillet. When lightly browned on both sides, pour in the Marsala, which should just cover the meat. Simmer until half of the wine has been absorbed. Add the broth, and simmer until the pan sauce is thickened. (If necessary, add a little more flour, bit by bit, until thickened to your taste.) Place onion and pepper slices on top of the scallops and sprinkle cheese all over. Cover the skillet. When cheese has melted, in about 1 minute, the dish is ready to serve. Accompany with fresh broccoli, corn-on-the-cob, green salad with avocado and Roquefort dressing, and a light dry wine. Makes 4 servings.

# DONNA SUMMER

# Summer Schnitzel

4 egg yolks
2 tablespoons milk
1 tablespoon minced parsley
¼ tablespoon onion salt
¼ teaspoon garlic salt
¼ teaspoon paprika
salt and pepper
4 pieces of veal, cut for Austrian
    schnitzel, about 6 ounces each
1 to 2 tablespoons flour
½ cup bread crumbs, grated from dried
    French bread
oil or margarine for sautéing
2 lemons

Beat egg yolks and milk together. Add parsley, onion and garlic salt, paprika, and salt and pepper to taste. Mix well, then let stand for 5 minutes. Stir again, then pour over the veal schnitzels in a shallow dish and let the meat soak for 10 to 15 minutes. Lift schnitzels from the egg mixture and coat lightly with flour, then with bread crumbs. Heat oil or margarine in a large skillet, and sauté schnitzels over low heat until golden brown. Cut lemons into lengthwise narrow wedges or strips and serve some with each portion of meat. Accompany with vegetables or salad. Makes 4 servings.

# EARL MOUNTBATTEN OF BURMA

# Leg of Venison with Peach Sauce

1 leg of venison, 7 to 8 pounds
1 tablespoon flour
1 tablespoon meat tenderizer
½ teaspoon salt
½ teaspoon black pepper
½ teaspoon paprika
½ teaspoon garlic salt
½ teaspoon ground ginger

1 cup beef or chicken stock
¼ pound butter (1 stick), melted
1 can (20 ounces) peeled peaches in syrup
1 cinnamon stick, 2 inches
1 tablespoon cornstarch or flour

Wipe venison with a damp cloth and put it on a rack in a roasting pan. Mix 1 tablespoon flour, the meat tenderizer and seasonings, and rub the mixture over the meat. Mix stock and melted butter. Roast venison in a preheated 350°F. oven, basting often with the butter mixture, for 3 hours. Remove to a well-heated platter and keep warm for 15 minutes. Reserve the pan drippings.

Simmer the peaches and syrup with the cinnamon stick for 15 minutes. Remove from heat, discard cinnamon, and mash peaches to a smooth purée. Skim excess fat from pan drippings. Mix cornstarch (or use flour) with a little cold water to make a smooth paste, and stir into the defatted drippings. Cook over low heat, stirring constantly, until the mixture thickens. Stir in the mashed peaches until smooth. Spoon some of the sauce over the venison, and serve the rest separately in a well-heated sauceboat. Makes 8 to 10 servings.

# PRESIDENT GERALD R. FORD

# Liver Deluxe

2 tablespoons butter
1 large onion, sliced thin
1 pound calf's liver, sliced thin
½ cup flour
2 cups brown gravy
chopped fresh parsley
salt and pepper
8 slices of bacon, fried crisp

Melt butter in a skillet and sauté onion slices until translucent. Push onion slices to the side. Coat slices of liver with flour and brown in the skillet on both sides. Pour gravy over liver, and sprinkle with chopped parsley and salt and pepper to taste. Simmer for 2 minutes. Arrange on a serving platter, and place bacon on top of liver. Makes 4 servings.

TOMÁS HELI CARDONA MEJIA

# Roast Leg of Lamb with Flageolets

1 can (10½ ounces) consommé
2 cups cold water
2 tablespoons butter
1 leg of lamb, 6 to 7 pounds

1 pound dried white pea beans
    or dried green flageolets,
    or 2 cans (1 pound each)
    flageolets

2 teaspoons salt
¼ teaspoon black pepper
3 garlic cloves, peeled
¼ cup tomato purée

juice of 1 lemon (optional)
¼ cup chopped fresh parsley
radish roses
watercress sprigs

If you are using dried beans, prepare these first. Wash and pick over beans. Place in a large saucepan, cover with cold water, and add the salt. Bring to a boil, then at once remove from heat and let the beans remain in the hot water for 1 hour. Add black pepper, 1 garlic clove put through a press, the tomato purée, consommé, 2 cups cold water and the butter. Again bring to a boil, reduce to a simmer, and continue cooking for 1½ hours, or until beans are tender but not mushy. Add more water as needed to keep beans covered at all times.

If you are using canned flageolets (they come packed in jars also), heat them just before the lamb is done, with 1 teaspoon salt, the black pepper, garlic and tomato purée.

Wipe the lamb with a damp cloth and cut off excess fat. Cut remaining 2 garlic cloves into slivers. Make deep incisions in the flesh of the leg and insert slivers of garlic. If you wish, rub lamb all over with the lemon juice. Let the lamb stand at room temperature for 1 hour before roasting. (It's even better if the lamb is left overnight to absorb the flavors of garlic and lemon, but it must be refrigerated if left overnight.) Place lamb, fat side up, on a rack in an open roasting pan. Roast in a preheated 325°F. oven for about 3 hours.

Transfer lamb to a serving platter and surround with flageolets. Sprinkle with parsley and garnish with radish roses and watercress sprigs. Makes 8 servings.

JOSEPHINE BAKER

# Saddle of Lamb Polignac

3 saddles of lamb (see Note)
1 tablespoon salt
1 tablespoon freshly ground black pepper
½ cup bread crumbs
1 pound fresh mushrooms, chopped fine
3 medium-size onions, minced to a purée
2 garlic cloves, peeled and put through
    a press
1 tablespoon minced fresh parsley

2 teaspoons tomato paste
½ teaspoon dry mustard
dash of Tabasco
½ pound truffles (see Note), sliced
3 medium-size onions, chopped fine
2½ to 3 cups Sauce Devine
    (recipe follows)

Preheat oven to 400°F. Rub the saddles well with the salt and pepper. Roast in the preheated oven for 30 minutes. Remove lamb from oven and cut each saddle into slices (loin chops), making them rather thick. Make a dressing with the bread crumbs and next 7 ingredients; mix well. Spread a little of the dressing on alternate slices of lamb and sandwich 2 slices together, fastening them with wooden food picks or small stainless-steel skewers.

In a shallow roasting pan make a bed of truffle slices and chopped onion, and arrange the stuffed lamb slices on top. Pour the sauce over. Return to the oven and roast until done to your taste. For pink lamb (as the French prefer it), roast for 30 minutes, then glaze under the broiler for just a few minutes. Or roast longer, to your taste. Makes 8 servings.

## Sauce Devine

2 tablespoons butter
3 tablespoons arrowroot
1 cup chicken broth
½ cup heavy cream
½ teaspoon Beau Monde seasoning

½ teaspoon monosodium glutamate
1 tablespoon minced fresh parsley
salt and white pepper
½ cup white wine
½ cup grated American cheese

Melt butter in a saucepan. Add arrowroot and mix well. Gradually stir in chicken broth. Bring to the boiling point and simmer, stirring often, until sauce is thickened. Stir in cream, seasoning and parsley, and add salt and pepper to taste. When smooth, add wine, finally the grated cheese. Remove from heat after adding cheese, and stir until cheese is melted. Use at once. Makes 2½ to 3 cups.

*Note:* Usually we think of the saddle as the double loin, but this name can also be used for a single loin roast, as is intended here. France has some smaller lambs than we generally find in our markets, so you may find 2 loin roasts ample for 8 servings. The loin roast is the most expensive cut for us to buy, but this recipe will work as well with other lamb chops.

Truffles are costly even in France, but here the price of ½ pound would be astronomical. Instead you could use more mushrooms, or mix parsley with the chopped onion for the vegetable bed in the roasting pan.

THE HONORABLE
DR. MARION MILL PREMINGER

# Lamb and Chicken Gabonais with Green Rice Ring

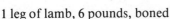

1 leg of lamb, 6 pounds, boned
3 broiler chickens, 2 pounds each, boned
4 large onions, peeled and chopped
4 green peppers, chopped
1 can (1 pound, 13 ounces) tomatoes
½ cup tomato purée
2 cups water
2 cups dry red wine
2 teaspoons salt

¼ teaspoon black pepper
¼ teaspoon cayenne pepper
¼ teaspoon Tabasco
¼ cup chopped truffles

Roast lamb and chickens in a 300°F. oven for 1½ hours, or until tender. Remove from roasting pan and keep warm. Skim excess fat from pan drippings. Braise onions and green peppers in the pan drippings. Add tomatoes, tomato purée, water and wine. Cook until vegetables are tender. Add seasonings and truffles. Slice lamb and chicken. Pour the sauce over lamb and chicken slices, and serve with green rice ring (recipe follows). Makes 16 servings.

## Green Rice Ring

2 cups uncooked rice
5 cups milk
2 tablespoons butter
2 tablespoons chopped onion
¼ cup chopped green pepper
2 tablespoons chopped parsley
2 tablespoons chopped pimiento
4 hard-cooked eggs, shelled and chopped
1 cup salted peanuts, chopped
1 raw egg, beaten
¼ teaspoon salt

114

Wash rice, drain, and mix with 4 cups of the milk in the top part of a large double boiler. Cook over boiling water, stirring occasionally, for 1 hour, or until rice is tender. Melt butter in a small pan and sauté onion and green pepper until tender. Stir into the rice, and add all remaining ingredients, including the last cup of milk. Mix well, then pack into a greased 9-inch ring mold that is deep enough to hold at least 2½ quarts. Bake in a 375°F. oven for 1 hour. Unmold, fill the center with buttered green beans, and garnish with parsley sprigs and radish roses. Makes 16 servings.

JUDY GARLAND

# Ham Casserole
# with Sherry

4 cups ground cooked ham
2 cups cooked rice
½ cup heavy cream
2 eggs, well beaten
2 tomatoes, peeled and chopped
2 tablespoons diced green pepper
1 tablespoon grated onion
1 teaspoon prepared mustard
1 teaspoon Worcestershire sauce
4 ounces sherry wine

Combine all ingredients, mixing them well. Put the mixture into a well-greased 2-quart casserole. Bake in a preheated 350°F. oven for 45 minutes. If you like, sprinkle the top with buttered bread crumbs and paprika. Makes 6 servings.

# LEROY NEIMAN

# Midnight Chops
for Two

2 pork chops, 1¼ to 1½ inches thick
½ cup bread crumbs
apple, celery, mushrooms, onions
oil
chopped parsley
milk

Chops should be thick for tender and juicy results. Trim chops; cut off bones and excess fat. Center a sharp thin knife between the flat sides of a chop about 2 inches from the side where the top bone was removed. Without enlarging the entrance hole, move the knife blade around to make a large pocket. Make a pocket in the second chop.

Make bread crumbs from a mixture of equal parts of corn bread, soda bread and good white bread. Peel and chop apple, wash and chop celery, trim and slice mushrooms, and chop onion, preparing enough of the combined ingredients to make about 1 cup of the mixture. Sauté these, in the smallest amount of oil needed, until tender. Sprinkle with parsley and mix with the bread crumbs. Add milk if necessary to moisten the stuffing. Fill the pockets in the chops, and sew up the openings with a heavy needle and coarse thread.

Sear the chops in a hot skillet, then transfer them to a baking pan. Cover pan and bake in a preheated 350°F. oven for 45 minutes to 1 hour, until done to your taste. Serve by candlelight. Makes 2 servings.

# ISIDORE NEWMAN II

# Choucroute

*This is Mr. Newman's favorite dish, so much so that he named his favorite horse after the dish.*

8 pounds sauerkraut
½ pound slab bacon
2 onions
4 garlic cloves
1 pound short ribs of beef
2½ pounds pork spareribs
1 tablespoon oil
2½ pounds pork tenderloin
20 juniper berries

12 peppercorns
1½ bottles dry Champagne
    or still white wine
2 bay leaves
1 teaspoon dried thyme
2 cups chicken stock
1 frying chicken, about 3 pounds
1 kielbasa (Polish sausage)
12 garlic frankfurters or knackwurst

Soak sauerkraut in cold water to cover for 5 to 6 hours. Drain well, then squeeze to remove remaining liquid. Cut slab bacon into cubes. Peel and chop onions. Peel and mince garlic, or put cloves through a press. Have beef ribs and pork ribs cracked. Put bacon cubes and oil in a large heavy pot. Add onions, garlic, beef ribs, spareribs and pork tenderloin. Cover and cook over low heat until meats are lightly browned; turn everything over occasionally. Crush juniper berries and peppercorns and add them to the kettle. Pour in ½ bottle of the wine and toss in bay leaves and thyme. Turn the meats over. Add chicken stock. By hand, add the sauerkraut, spreading it all over the top of the meats. Bring the liquids to a full boil on top of the stove, then reduce to a simmer and cook over low heat for 1 hour.

Transfer the contents of the kettle to a large casserole. Cut the chicken into serving pieces and add to the rest. Cover casserole and bake in a preheated 350°F. oven for 45 minutes. Slice the kielbasa. Remove casserole from oven and add frankfurters or knackwurst and sliced kielbasa, and pour in remaining wine. Return to oven and bake for 45 minutes longer. The longer you cook *choucroute*, the better it is. If you plan to cook it longer, wait to add the sausages until 20 minutes before the end of cooking.

Arrange sauerkraut in the center of a heated large serving platter, and spoon the pan sauce over it. Arrange the meats, sliced as needed, around it. Accompany with boiled potatoes and baby carrots, and serve beer, white still wine or Champagne. Makes 12 servings.

# MRS. GERRI MAJOR

# Choucroute Garnie

2 cans (27 ounces each) sauerkraut
2 tablespoons sesame oil
½ cup thin slices of carrot
1 cup thin slices of onion
1 teaspoon caraway seeds
1 bay leaf
1 teaspoon crushed red pepper
12 peppercorns
12 juniper berries
½ tablespoon minced fresh parsley
1 can (10½ ounces) beef bouillon
2 cups beer
salt

6 smoked pork chops
½ pound chunk bacon
1 cervelat sausage
1 unsmoked veal sausage
3 Kosher frankfurters

Drain sauerkraut, place in a large bowl, cover with cold water, and soak for 5 minutes. Drain well, then pick up large handfuls at a time and squeeze well to remove remaining liquid. Pour sesame oil into a 3-quart casserole, add carrot and onion, and simmer until vegetables are tender but not browned. Stir in sauerkraut, caraway seeds, bay leaf, crushed red pepper, peppercorns, juniper berries, parsley, bouillon, beer, and salt to taste. Cover and bring to a boil on top of the stove. Transfer casserole to a preheated 325°F. oven and cook for 3 hours. If sauerkraut becomes dry, add more beer.

About 2½ hours before serving, add the smoked chops and the chunk bacon. About 30 minutes before serving, add cervelat sausage, veal sausage and frankfurters. Remove finished *choucroute* from the oven and let it stand for 5 minutes.

Place sauerkraut in the center of a large platter and arrange chops and sliced sausages and bacon around it. Serve 1 chop, a slice of the sausages and a slice of bacon with each portion. Accompany with boiled potatoes dusted with caraway seeds. Makes 6 servings.

119

# ERICA WILSON

# Toad in a Hole

1 cup flour
2 eggs
1 cup milk
¾ teaspoon salt
pepper
1 pound sausages

Preheat oven to 400°F. Combine flour, eggs, milk, salt, and pepper to taste in a blender container and whirl until well mixed. Cook sausages over moderate heat until done to your taste. Arrange sausages in a 6-cup baking dish and sprinkle drippings over them. Pour batter over them. Bake in the preheated oven for 30 minutes, or until pudding has risen and is crisp and brown. Makes 4 servings.

MRS. RUTH H. JONES

# Kallaloo with Fungi

*This dish is a specialty of St. Thomas in the*
*Virgin Islands.*

1 pound pigs' tails
1 pound pigs' feet
1 pound ham
1 pound ham hocks
1 small onion, peeled and minced
2 tablespoons minced celery
1 parsley sprig

¼ teaspoon dried thyme
hot pepper
2 eggplants, about 10 ounces each
1 ½ pounds fresh fish (redman, porgy or
    yellowtail snapper), dressed
1 dozen fresh okra, washed
2 pounds fresh kale or spinach, washed
lime juice

Soak pigs' tails, pigs' feet, ham and ham hocks in water to cover overnight, to remove excess salt. Next day clean well, cover with fresh water, and boil until tender. Remove meats, but leave cooking water in the kettle. Discard bones and cut meat into pieces. Put onion, celery, parsley, thyme, and hot pepper to taste in the kettle. Cook for a few minutes. Peel and dice eggplants. Add eggplant to the kettle and cook until tender.

Boil fish in enough water to cover until just done. Remove fish from the pot, but save the cooking water. Remove bones from fish and flake the flesh. Strain the cooking water into the kettle with the eggplant. Add okra and kale or spinach to the kettle and cook for 15 minutes. Add flaked fish, the meats, and lime juice to taste. Cook for 5 minutes. Serve with fungi (recipe follows). Makes 6 servings.

## Fungi

4 cups water
2 ounces butter or margarine
½ tablespoon salt
2 cups cornmeal

Bring water to a boil with half of the butter. Add salt and slowly stir in cornmeal. Stir in remaining butter, and cook the mixture over gentle heat, stirring constantly, until it leaves the sides of the pan. Remove from heat and serve hot or cold. To serve with kallaloo, drop tablespoons of fungi into the kettle, and eat both together. Makes 6 to 8 servings.

121

# 7

## VEGETABLES AND RICE

# Ratatouille

3 large onions
1 eggplant, about 1 pound
4 zucchini, about 6 ounces each
2 yellow summer squashes, about
    8 ounces each
6 medium-size tomatoes
4 green peppers
¼ cup olive oil
3 garlic cloves, peeled
salt and pepper

Peel onions and chop fine. Wash and trim eggplant, zucchini and yellow squashes, and cut into ¼-inch slices. Wash tomatoes and cut into thin slices. Wash and trim green peppers, and cut into strips. Heat oil in a 3-quart casserole with a heavy lid. Push garlic through a press into the oil and cook, covered, for about 3 minutes. Add onions, cover, and cook for about 10 minutes. Add the other vegetables in layers, sprinkling each layer with salt and pepper. When casserole is filled, cover, and bake in a preheated 350°F. oven for 45 minutes. Serve from the casserole. This is good hot or cold. Makes 8 servings.

THE HONORABLE
PIERRE ELLIOT TRUDEAU

# Batter-Fried Vegetables

Prepare a platter of bite-size vegetables.

carrots, cut on the diagonal
1-inch pieces of green or red bell peppers
onion rings
green beans
whole mushrooms

Refrigerate vegetables until really cold. Make the batter (recipe follows). Heat light cooking oil to 375°F. on a frying thermometer, or until heat haze rises from the surface. Dip vegetables, one at a time, into cold batter, and put about 10 vegetable pieces at a time into the hot oil. Cook for 1 to 3 minutes, just until vegetables are crisp. Drain on paper towels, then serve at once with light soy dipping sauce and grated fresh gingerroot. Be sure oil is once again heated to 375°F. before continuing to cook.

## Batter

1 egg yolk
2 cups ice-cold water
1⅔ cups flour
⅛ teaspoon baking powder

Drop egg yolk into a bowl. With a whisk beat in the ice-cold water. Sift flour and baking powder together and whisk into the bowl until well mixed. Batter may be a little lumpy. Use at once, very cold. Makes about 2 cups batter, enough for vegetables for 6 servings.

# Eggplant Provençale

Choose a firm eggplant. Wash and peel it, and cut into ½-inch slices. Sprinkle slices with salt, pepper and paprika, then with a mixture of minced parsley, minced garlic and bread crumbs. Shake a few drops of oil over the slices. Place in a single layer on a lightly oiled baking sheet.

Choose enough medium-size tomatoes to equal half of the eggplant slices. Wash tomatoes and cut into halves. Sprinkle cut sides with salt and pepper, then with a mixture of minced parsley, minced garlic and bread crumbs. Shake a few drops of oil over the halves. Place on another lightly oiled baking sheet.

Grill eggplant and tomatoes in the broiler or bake in a preheated 375°F. oven until lightly browned and tender. To serve, place a tomato half on each eggplant slice. A fat 1-pound eggplant will give you 10 to 12 slices. With 5 or 6 tomatoes, this will make 4 to 6 servings.

# A. PHILIP RANDOLPH

# Baked Beans

2 pounds dried beans
1 teaspoon salt
1½ cups brown sugar
3 tablespoons prepared mustard
3 tablespoons Worcestershire sauce
⅓ cup sweet pickle juice
3 garlic cloves, peeled
½ pound lean and fat salt pork

Use kidney beans, Navy beans or soybeans; I use Navy beans. Pour beans into a large bowl, with room to expand, and cover with cold water. Soak beans for 6 hours. Pour off soaking water and lift beans into a large pot. Add 4 cups fresh water, enough to cover beans, add the salt, and bring to a boil. Reduce to a simmer and cook over very low heat for 2 hours. Turn beans into a 2½-quart bean pot or other heavy casserole.

Mix sugar, mustard, Worcestershire and pickle juice, and push garlic through a press into the mixture. Stir gently into the beans. Cut the salt pork down the center, and bury the 2 pieces in the beans. Cover the pot, and bake in a preheated 300°F. oven for 6 hours. Uncover pot and bake for 1 more hour, to brown the top. Makes 6 servings, or more.

# Peas Braised with Lettuce and Onions

1 firm fresh head of lettuce
½ cup water
3 ounces butter
1 ½ tablespoons sugar
½ teaspoon salt
2 tablespoons minced mint leaves
2 tablespoons minced fresh parsley
3 pounds tender green peas, shelled
12 green onions (scallions),
     white bulb ends only
1 tablespoon arrowroot
1 cup white wine

Wash lettuce carefully and drain well; cut the head into quarters. Put water, butter, sugar, salt, mint and parsley in a heavy saucepan, and bring to a boil. Add peas and bulb portion of the onions, and toss all together lightly. Arrange lettuce quarters on top and baste with some of the liquid in the pan. Cover and cook over low heat for 30 minutes, or until tender. During cooking remove cover several times and add 1 or 2 tablespoons water if it is needed.

Just before serving stir arrowroot into wine and add to the peas. Cook just long enough to heat wine and thicken the liquid slightly. Turn into a vegetable dish, arranging peas and onions in the center and placing lettuce quarters around the edge. Makes 6 servings.

SAUNDRA SHARP

# French-Fried Cauliflower with Minted Peas

## Minted Peas

2 pounds fresh peas, or 2 packages
    (10 ounces each) frozen peas
1 teaspoon dried mint
1 teaspoon chopped parsley

½ teaspoon salt
½ teaspoon pepper
¼ teaspoon sugar
2 tablespoons butter, melted

Shell fresh peas and cook them; or cook frozen peas; drain, but leave in the saucepan. Add mint, parsley, salt, pepper and sugar, then the melted butter. Toss lightly to mix. Keep warm until ready to spoon into the center of the cauliflower.

## French-Fried Cauliflower

1 head of cauliflower, 1 to 1¼ pounds
½ cup fine bread crumbs
1 egg, beaten with 1 tablespoon water
oil or shortening for deep-frying
salt and pepper

Trim cauliflower, then parboil for 10 minutes. Cool. Separate the head into flowerets. Dip each piece into bread crumbs, then into the beaten egg, then again into bread crumbs. Heat oil or shortening to 370°F. on a frying thermometer, and deep-fry the flowerets until golden brown. Transfer briefly to paper towels, then sprinkle with salt and pepper and arrange in a ring on a well-heated platter. Spoon minted peas in the center and serve at once. Makes 8 servings.

# IRVING GOLDMAN

# Green Beans Gourmet

2 pounds fresh green snap beans
1 medium-size onion
1 garlic clove
4 celery ribs
1 teaspoon sugar
½ teaspoon salt
¼ teaspoon freshly ground black pepper
¼ teaspoon cayenne pepper
¼ teaspoon ground allspice
1 lemon
2 tablespoons butter
½ cup grated blanched almonds or
    hazelnuts

Wash beans, remove tops and tails, and place in a large saucepan. Add 1½ cups water, bring to a boil, and cook beans until just tender; do not overcook them, they should still be crisp. Drain the cooking liquid into another large saucepan, and cover beans with very cold water to stop the cooking and set the green color. Drain beans again and set aside.

While beans cook, peel and chop onion; peel and mince garlic; wash celery and cut into julienne strips. Drop these vegetables into the saucepan of bean cooking liquid, and add sugar, salt and spices. Grate lemon rind into the mixture, then extract lemon juice and add it; there should be about 2 tablespoons juice. Bring the mixture to a boil, then simmer, covered, for 20 minutes, until celery and onion are tender. Add beans to the saucepan and place over heat until beans are hot again. Stir in butter; when it is melted, serve the beans, sprinkled with the grated almonds or hazelnuts. Makes 6 to 8 servings.

# BARBARA WALTERS

# My Mother's Stuffed Cabbage Rolls

3 pounds lean beef chuck, ground
2 teaspoons salt
¾ teaspoon pepper
2 teaspoons celery salt
½ cup ketchup
2 eggs
½ cup crushed unsalted crackers
2 heads (2 pounds each) green cabbage

oil for baking pan
3 cups chopped onions
3 cups chili sauce
1½ cups grape jelly

In a large bowl combine beef, seasonings, ketchup, eggs and crushed crackers. Mix with the hands just until mixture is well combined. Cut out and discard the hard center core of the cabbages. Place cabbages in a large kettle and pour boiling water over them. Let them stand until leaves are flexible and can easily be removed from the head, about 5 minutes. If necessary, return cabbage to hot water to soften inner leaves.

Preheat oven to 375°F. Using a ½-cup measure, scoop up scant ½-cup portions of the meat mixture. With hands form into rolls 3 inches long and 1 inch wide. Make about 28 rolls altogether. Place each roll on a drained cabbage leaf. Fold top of leaf over stuffing, then fold in the sides, then roll up into an oblong package. Continue until all stuffing is used. Oil a roasting pan 12 x 11½ x 2¼ inches. Spread chopped onions evenly on the bottom. Arrange cabbage rolls in neat rows on top of onions. Combine chili sauce and grape jelly with ¼ cup water in a large saucepan. Heat over medium heat, stirring, until jelly is melted. Pour sauce over cabbage rolls and cover pan tightly with foil. Bake in the preheated oven for 2 hours. Remove foil and brush tops of rolls with sauce from bottom of pan. Bake uncovered for 40 minutes longer, until sauce is thick and syrupy and cabbage rolls are glazed. Serve with sauce spooned over the rolls. Makes 14 servings, 2 rolls per serving.

HOWARD SAMUELS

# Spanakopita (Greek Spinach Pies)

## Pastry

2 cups sifted flour
1 egg
1 tablespoon olive oil
½ teaspoon salt
6 tablespoons ice water
2 cups oil for deep-frying

Sift flour into a bowl and make a well in the center. Drop egg, olive oil and salt into the well and mix well with a fork. Add the water, little by little, with a fork stirring the flour into the liquid mixture until you have a workable dough. Turn out on a floured board and knead well. Divide dough into 12 even-size pieces, shape each one into a ball, and cover with a damp towel to prevent drying.

## Filling

1½ pounds fresh spinach
1 cup chopped scallions (green onions)
1 teaspoon salt
½ cup chopped fresh dill
½ pound feta cheese, crumbled
1 teaspoon freshly ground black pepper
½ cup oil

Wash spinach thoroughly, drain, and dry well. Chop with the scallions. Add salt and continue to chop. Let spinach mixture stand for 15 minutes, then squeeze to extract most of the accumulated liquid. Add dill, cheese, pepper and ½ cup oil, and blend well.

Roll out the dough, 1 piece at a time, on a lightly floured board into a thin round pancake. Place 1 heaping tablespoon of filling in the center of each round, and fold edges together to enclose filling, pressing the edges to seal. When all the pies are prepared, deep-fry them in the hot oil until golden and puffy. Makes 12 servings.

132

# SHIRLEY MACLAINE

# Stuffed Green Peppers

13 large green peppers
1 cup uncooked wild rice
1 large onion
2 garlic cloves
3 parsley sprigs
2 ounces butter
½ cup chopped mushrooms
1 teaspoon salt
1 teaspoon black pepper
1½ cups canned tomato paste (12 ounces)
½ cup beef broth

1½ pounds ground beef
1 cup white wine
butter for baking dish
grated Parmesan cheese (optional)

Buy fresh-looking green peppers with shiny skins and no blemishes. Use 12 peppers for stuffing. Cut off the tops and set these aside. Scoop out ribs and seeds, wash peppers well, and set upside down to drain. Cook the wild rice until just tender; set aside. Peel onion and chop to fine bits; peel and mince garlic; trim the extra green pepper, discard ribs and seeds, and chop; wash and chop parsley.

Melt the butter in a saucepan over low heat and in it sauté onion, garlic and mushrooms until golden. Add chopped green pepper and parsley, salt and pepper, tomato paste and beef broth. Mix, then cover and cook for 10 minutes. Set aside to cool slightly.

Preheat oven to 350°F. Mix ground beef with cooked rice, tossing with a fork. Add the seasoned sauce and ½ cup of the wine and mix well together. Stuff peppers with the mixture, and arrange them in a single layer close together in a well-buttered baking dish that will just hold them. Top the stuffing layer with a sprinkle of grated cheese, if you like. Cover the peppers with the cut-off tops. Pour remaining ½ cup wine into the dish and cover tightly (if baking dish has no cover, use heavy-duty foil). Bake in the preheated oven for 1 hour. When serving, transfer peppers carefully to a platter and spoon pan sauce over them. Makes 12 servings.

## MRS. YITZHAK RABIN

# Stuffed Green Peppers in Tomato Sauce

2 large onions
¼ cup oil
1 pound meat, chopped
1 cup uncooked rice
1 egg, slightly beaten
2 tablespoons water
1 tablespoon chopped fresh parsley
salt and pepper

8 to 10 large green peppers
8 ounces tomato sauce
⅔ cup water
juice of 1 lemon
1 teaspoon sugar

Peel and chop 1 onion, and sauté it in 2 tablespoons of the oil in a large skillet until golden. Add the meat and sauté, stirring all the while with a wooden spoon, until all red color has disappeared. Spoon meat and onion into a bowl and add rice, egg, 2 tablespoons water, parsley and salt and pepper to taste. Mix well.

Wash peppers; carefully cut off the tops and reserve them. Trim away all ribs and seeds without damaging the pepper shells. Fill each pepper two-thirds full of the stuffing (rice will expand as it cooks). Cover peppers with the reserved tops. Arrange them in a single layer close together in a deep heatproof glass or ceramic baking dish or casserole with a cover.

Chop the second onion and sauté in remaining oil in a saucepan until golden. Add tomato sauce, ⅔ cup water, lemon juice, sugar, and salt and pepper to taste. Simmer for 10 minutes. Pour sauce over stuffed peppers, and cover the baking dish. Bake in a preheated 350° F. oven for about 40 minutes. Makes 8 to 10 servings.

# DEBBY BOONE

# Vegetarian Tacos

Cover ½ cup uncooked millet with 1 cup water, bring to a boil, then simmer for about 30 minutes, until millet is soft. Flavor it with a little soy sauce. Shred lettuce, grate cheese, peel and chop onions, wash and chop tomatoes, preparing amounts to taste. Mash a peeled avocado and mix in chopped onions. Heat 12 corn tortillas, in the oven, or by steaming over water. Place some of all ingredients in each warm tortilla and fold them over into taco form. With 12 tortillas and ½ cup millet, you can make 4 servings.

BILLIE JEAN KING

# Rice Casserole with Cheese

¼ pound butter or margarine (1 stick)
1 cup chopped onions
4 cups freshly cooked rice, hot
2 cups dairy sour cream
1 cup cottage cheese
1 large bay leaf, crumbled
½ teaspoon salt
⅛ teaspoon pepper
2 cans (4 ounces each) green chili peppers
2 cups grated natural sharp cheese
chopped fresh parsley

Preheat oven to 375°F. Use a little of the butter to coat a 2-quart baking dish, 12 x 8 inches. Melt remaining butter in a large skillet and sauté onions until golden brown. Remove skillet from heat and stir in hot rice, the sour cream, cottage cheese, bay leaf, salt and pepper. Toss lightly and mix well. Layer half of the rice mixture in the buttered baking dish. Slit open the green chilies and rinse out seeds. Chop chilies, and spread half of them over the rice mixture, then add half of the grated cheese. Repeat with the rest of the ingredients. Bake uncovered for 25 minutes, or until casserole is hot and bubbly. Sprinkle with parsley and serve. Makes 6 to 8 servings.

## Fluffy Rice

Bring 2½ cups cold water to a boil in a large saucepan. Add 1 cup converted rice and 1 teaspoon salt. Bring again to a boil, reduce to a simmer, cover tightly, and cook over low heat for about 25 minutes, or until all water is absorbed. Makes 4 cups.

SIR ARTHUR AND
LADY CICELY GOODHART

# Rice Pilaff with Chicken Livers

2 tablespoons chicken fat, butter or oil
1 large onion, peeled and chopped
2 garlic cloves, peeled and minced
1 cup chopped mushrooms
1 bay leaf
½ pound fresh chicken livers, chopped
½ cup finely chopped blanched almonds
1 large green pepper, trimmed and chopped

¼ teaspoon dried thyme
1 teaspoon salt
pepper
1½ cups uncooked rice
1½ cups chicken broth
1½ cups hot water
butter for casserole
½ pound sharp cheese, grated

Melt fat in a large heavy saucepan. Add onion, garlic, mushrooms and bay leaf, cover, and cook over low heat for 10 minutes. Add chopped chicken livers, almonds, green pepper, thyme, salt, and pepper to taste. Stir gently over low heat for 5 minutes. Wash rice well, and drain. Add rice to the saucepan with chicken broth and water. Stir, then bring to a boil. Check the seasoning and adjust if necessary. Cover the saucepan and simmer for 5 minutes.

Butter a 2-quart casserole with a cover. Spoon rice mixture into casserole and cover. Bake in a preheated 375°F. oven for 45 minutes. Remove cover and sprinkle the cheese on top. Return to oven until cheese is lightly browned. Makes 8 servings.

# PAULINE TRIGÈRE

# Rice Pauline

2 large onions
2 ounces butter
½ tablespoon salt
freshly ground pepper
2 pounds fresh mushrooms
2 cups heavy cream
dash of grated nutmeg
3 to 4 cups cooked rice, hot

Peel and slice onions. Melt half of the butter in a large skillet and add onions, salt, and pepper to taste. Sauté onions over low heat until they are "light blond" (as Miss Trigère describes it), which will take about 30 minutes. Remove onions to a separate pan or bowl. While onions cook, wash and trim mushrooms, roll in a towel to dry, then slice mushrooms. Melt remaining butter in the same skillet and sauté mushrooms until tender, about 10 minutes. Test with a fork. Combine onions and mushrooms.

About 5 minutes before dinner, pour the cream into the warm onions and mushrooms. Bring just to the boiling point. Just before serving taste, and correct seasoning if necessary. Add a dash of nutmeg. Mix sauce with cooked rice at the stove, or right at the table as Miss Trigère does. Mix thoroughly. Makes 6 servings.

*Note:* The onion-mushroom-cream sauce can be used for spaghetti or noodles, or for leftover meat.

HAL HACKETT

# Peanut Rice (Orez Botneem)

*"This is a typical Israeli accompaniment
for a chicken dish."*

2 tablespoons grated onion
2 tablespoons butter or margarine
2 tablespoons honey
1 teaspoon Worcestershire sauce
1 teaspoon dry mustard
½ tablespoon salt
1 can (4 ounces) sliced mushrooms
2 cups uncooked rice
4½ cups water
½ teaspoon ground ginger
1 tablespoon minced parsley
butter for mold
1 cup soft bread crumbs
1½ cups coarsely chopped shelled peanuts

Lightly brown the onion in 1 tablespoon of the butter in a large deep skillet. Add honey, Worcestershire, mustard, salt and mushrooms; mix well. Add rice, water, ginger, parsley and remaining butter. Bring liquid to a boil, reduce to a simmer, and cook in the skillet for 20 to 30 minutes. Butter a 9-inch ring mold that holds about 2½ quarts. Coat the mold with soft bread crumbs. Pack the rice mixture into the mold and cover with remaining crumbs, then lightly cover with foil. Set the mold in a larger pan containing 2 inches of boiling water. Bake in a preheated 350°F. oven for 45 minutes.

Remove mold from oven and let it stand on top of the stove for 10 minutes. Unmold on a large serving platter and fill the center with fresh green beans sprinkled with nutmeg. Sprinkle with peanuts just before serving. Arrange the poultry main dish around the ring. Serve rice in wedges with any sauce from the poultry. Makes 8 servings.

# THE HONORABLE MORARJI R. DESAI

प्रधान मंत्री सचिवालय
PRIME MINISTER'S SECRETARIAT OFFICE

नई दिल्ली-११००११
NEW DELHI-110011

29th August, 1977

Dear Madam,

      The Prime Minister has received your letter of the 10th August in which you have asked for information about his favourite recipe for inclusion in your cookbook. The Prime Minister has no favourite recipe. His diet is simple and frugal, though somewhat unusual. He is a pure vegetarian and does not consume any cereals, pulses, beverages and cooked or raw vegetables. He has a breakfast consisting of a glass of boiled water and carrot juice (alternatively tender coconut water), with salt and pepper. For lunch and dinner, he has five pieces of raw garlic, half a litre of lukewarm cow's milk with honey, some fresh cheese prepared from cow's milk, dryfruits, cucumber and Indian sweets made with cow's milk and jaggery. He avoids sugar.

      A copy of his photograph is sent herewith, as desired.

Yours faithfully,

Mrs. Maria Adams Bell,
Founder-President,
The Educational Guild,
156/20 Riverside Drive
West New York,
New York 10032 (212) 927-8937

(N.S. Sreeraman)
Private Secretary to
the Prime Minister

140

# 8

## SALADS

## HENRY FORD II

# French Dressing

6 cups salad oil
1⅓ cups red-wine vinegar
1 cup cider vinegar
½ onion, peeled and minced
1 garlic clove, peeled and
    put through a press
2 tablespoons sugar
1 tablespoon prepared French mustard
2 dashes of Worcestershire sauce
fresh parsley sprigs
snipped fresh chives
salt and pepper

Put first 8 ingredients in a blender container. Add as much parsley and chives as you like. Blend until smooth. Add salt and pepper to taste. Other *fines herbes* can be added to your taste. This dressing will keep indefinitely if refrigerated. Makes about 8 cups.

    Unless you have a very large blender, you will need to process this a half or a third at a time.

# THE HONORABLE
# DAVID N. DINKINS

# Avocado Stuffed with Crab Meat

1 pound fresh crab meat
1 cup diced celery
1 teaspoon Worcestershire sauce
½ teaspoon salt
¼ teaspoon white pepper
¾ cup mayonnaise
2 large ripe avocados
4 strips of pimiento
4 strips of green pepper
crisp lettuce leaves
½ lemon, cut into 4 wedges
2 hard-cooked eggs, peeled and
    cut into wedges

Mix crab meat with celery, seasonings and mayonnaise. Peel avocados with a stainless-steel or silver knife. Carefully halve them and remove pits. Divide crab salad among the avocado halves and garnish each with a pimiento and green-pepper strip. Cover 4 glass salad plates with lettuce leaves, arrange an avocado half on each plate, and decorate with a lemon wedge and several egg wedges. Makes 4 servings.

THE HONORABLE
PATRICIA ROBERTS HARRIS

# Tropical Island Luncheon Salad

*This elegant salad is perfect for a summer buffet meal, lovely for a party. Garnish with herbs, greens, fruits and flowers.*

## I.  Honeydew Melon with Chicken Salad

1 cup chopped cooked chicken
1 cup chopped celery hearts
1 cup seedless grapes
¼ cup French dressing
¼ cup heavy cream
¼ cup mayonnaise
½ cup blanched almonds, chopped
1 apple, chopped
1 ripe honeydew melon

Marinate chicken, celery and grapes in French dressing for several hours; drain. Whip cream and fold in mayonnaise. Add to drained chicken mixture, and fold in almonds and apple. Halve melon, scoop out seeds, and fill hollows with chicken salad.

## II. Persian Melon with Crab Salad

1 pound cooked crab meat
½ teaspoon salt
¼ teaspoon white pepper
dash of Worcestershire sauce
1 cup diced celery
¾ cup mayonnaise
1 ripe Persian melon
strips of green pepper
strips of pimiento

Mix crab meat, seasonings, celery and mayonnaise. Halve melon, scoop out seeds, and fill hollows with crab salad. Garnish with strips of pepper and pimiento.

144

## III. Cantaloupe with Shrimp Salad

1 ½ cups chopped cooked shrimps
1 cup chopped celery
¼ cup chopped pitted olives
1 tablespoon minced onion
2 tablespoons prepared hot mustard
2 tablespoons prepared horseradish
⅓ cup French dressing
½ cup mayonnaise
1 ripe cantaloupe

Mix shrimps with next 5 ingredients, stir in French dressing, and fold in mayonnaise. Refrigerate for 1 hour. Halve cantaloupe, scoop out seeds, and fill hollows with shrimp salad.

Arrange all the melon halves on a large platter and decorate with blueberries, grapes, 1 large gardenia and pink apple blossoms. Sprinkle all over with grated fresh coconut. Serve with pink Champagne. Each melon half can be divided into 2 or 3 portions.

JOHN DENVER

# Annie Denver's Mandarin Tossed Salad

½ cup blanched almonds
2 tablespoons sugar
1 can (11 ounces) mandarin oranges
½ head of lettuce
2 scallions (green onions)

1 cup chopped celery
1 tablespoon minced parsley

Put almonds and sugar in a small heavy pan and cook over low heat, stirring all the time, until sugar is dissolved and almonds caramelized. Remove almonds from heat and let them cool. Drain mandarin oranges (syrup can be used for another recipe). Shred lettuce and chop scallions including green tops. Mix all ingredients together. Toss with dressing (recipe follows). Makes 4 servings.

## Dressing

½ cup salad oil
2 tablespoons vinegar
2 tablespoons sugar
½ teaspoon salt
dash of black pepper

Put all ingredients in a jar and shake vigorously until sugar and salt are dissolved. Makes ¾ cup.

146

MARTHA SLEEPER

# Mushroom
# and
# Spinach Salad

10 ounces fresh spinach
6 strips of bacon
1 bunch of scallions (green onions),
    about 10
¼ pound fresh raw mushrooms
6 tablespoons olive oil
2 tablespoons lemon juice

1 raw egg yolk
1 garlic clove
¾ teaspoon salt
¼ teaspoon sugar
⅛ teaspoon black pepper
⅛ teaspoon dry mustard

Wash spinach thoroughly, trim, and remove any coarse or damaged leaves and all stems. Roll leaves in a towel to dry, then place leaves in a large salad bowl. Broil bacon until crisp, drain, and cool. Crumble over the spinach. Wash and trim scallions, and cut into thin crosswise slices. Wash mushrooms and pat dry; cut into thin slices. Add scallions and raw mushrooms to spinach and chill the salad.

Beat oil, lemon juice and egg yolk to mix well. Peel garlic and put through a press into dressing. Add the seasonings, blend well, and chill. At serving time toss dressing with salad. Makes 6 servings.

# 9

## BREADS

NAT "KING" COLE

# Real French Bread

1 package active dry yeast
2 cups warm water (105° to 115°F.)
4 cups sifted all-purpose flour
1 tablespoon sugar
2 teaspoons salt
melted butter

Dissolve yeast in 1 cup of the water. Sift flour, sugar and salt together into a large bowl and stir in dissolved yeast. Add just enough of the second cup of water to hold dough together. Mix until you have a soft, sticky dough. Cover bowl with a clean cloth and set it in a warm place, 80° to 85°F., to rise until doubled in size, from 2 to 4 hours.

When dough is high and spongy, punch it down with your fist and give it a good sound beating with your hand. Divide dough into 2 parts and place each one in a greased 6-inch round baking dish or heatproof glass casserole. Cover again, and let dough rise until it reaches the top of the dish.

Preheat oven to 400°F. Brush tops of loaves with melted butter, and bake for 1 hour. Makes 2 loaves.

150

# DR. AND MRS. BILLY GRAHAM

# Home-Baked Bread

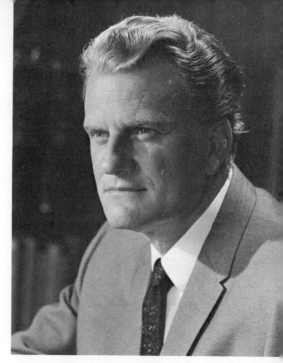

2 cups lukewarm water (105° to 115°F.)
1 package dry yeast
1 teaspoon salt
2 teaspoons sugar
5 cups unbleached flour
oil or butter for bowl
cornmeal or sesame seeds for baking sheet

Pour water into a large bowl and add yeast, salt and sugar. Stir to dissolve the dry ingredients, then let yeast become bubbly. Stir in 4 cups of the flour and mix into a dough. Turn out on a board or countertop and knead for 10 minutes, adding in remaining flour if necessary to make a dough that is not sticky, but smooth and elastic. Wash the bowl, coat it with oil or butter, and place the ball of dough in it, turning it around to oil all sides. Cover and let rise in a warm place, 80° to 85°F., until doubled in bulk, about 1 hour.

Turn out the dough and divide into 2 or 4 pieces. Shape each piece into a loaf. Loaves can be baked in oiled bread pans; for 2 loaves use pans 9 x 5 x 3 inches; for 4 loaves use pans 5 x 3 x 2 inches. Or they can be placed on a baking sheet. No oiling is needed for a sheet with nonstick coating, but plain baking sheets should be sprinkled with cornmeal or sesame seeds to prevent sticking. Score the top of each loaf 4 or 5 times with a sharp knife. Brush each loaf with water. Let them stand for 30 minutes, until well risen.

Preheat oven to 350°F. and place a pan of water on the bottom shelf. This will make steam while loaves are baking, and will help to make the crust crusty and delicious. Bake loaves for 45 minutes to 1 hour, until brown on the top.

To make whole-wheat bread, use 5 cups whole-wheat flour and 1 cup unbleached flour, and use 2 packages of yeast.

## ALEASE LAVALLIAS ADAMS

# My Mother's Holiday Bread —Hallah

5 heaping cups flour
1 cake compressed fresh yeast
3 tablespoons sugar
½ cup lukewarm water (80° to 90°F.)
2 tablespoons oil
½ tablespoon salt
¼ teaspoon grated nutmeg
1 egg
1 cup water
1 egg yolk
caraway seeds

Dump the flour onto a board or countertop, and make a well in the center. Crumble the yeast into the well and add 1 tablespoon of the sugar. Pour in the lukewarm water. Sprinkle some of the flour from the edges of the well into the yeast mixture; stir. Let stand for a few hours to allow the yeast mixture to rise within the circle of flour.

Add the oil and salt, sprinkle in the nutmeg, and finally add the whole egg and remaining 2 tablespoons sugar. Add 1 cup of water and mix all the ingredients together until flour is completely incorporated. Let the dough rise again for 30 minutes. Lightly flour a board or other smooth surface. Turn the dough onto it and knead for about 10 minutes, until dough is fairly hard. Form into 2 loaves and put into oiled baking pans, 9 x 5 x 3 inches. Let dough rise in the pans for 30 minutes. With hands gently brush cold water evenly over tops of loaves. Beat egg yolk with 1 tablespoon water and brush over loaves. Sprinkle with caraway seeds. Bake in a preheated 375°F. oven for 1 hour. Makes 2 loaves.

*Variations:* For onion bread, grate 1 onion and knead it into the dough just before shaping the loaves.

For braided *hallah* (the traditional shape), divide dough into 4 parts, and roll three of them into long strips. Make a long braid with these strips. Divide the last part into 3 portions and roll these into strips. Make a small braid with these and place it down the center of the large braid. Press it firmly into place and seal ends together, or tuck them into the grooves of the large braid.

VICE PRESIDENT AND
MRS. WALTER F. MONDALE

# Pumpkin Bread

1 ⅔ cups all-purpose flour
1 ½ cups sugar
1 teaspoon baking soda
¼ teaspoon baking powder
¾ teaspoon salt
½ teaspoon ground cloves
½ teaspoon ground cinnamon

½ teaspoon grated nutmeg
2 eggs
1 cup puréed pumpkin, fresh or canned
½ cup oil
½ cup water
½ cup chopped nuts
½ cup chopped dates

Preheat oven to 350°F. Sift first 8 ingredients together into a large bowl. Add eggs, pumpkin, oil and water, and beat with a rotary beater until well mixed. Stir in nuts and dates. Spoon batter into a large loaf pan, 9 x 5 x 3 inches, lined with nonstick coating. Bake for 1½ hours.

# ROBERT REDFORD

## Lola's Whole-Wheat Quick Bread

1 egg, beaten
2 cups buttermilk
3 tablespoons molasses or honey
1½ tablespoons melted butter
2 cups whole-wheat flour
1 teaspoon baking soda
2 teaspoons baking powder
½ teaspoon salt
½ cup shelled walnuts
½ cup raisins

Preheat oven to 400°F. Combine beaten egg with buttermilk, molasses or honey, and butter. Mix all dry ingredients together and mix with buttermilk mixture. Stir in walnuts and raisins. Spoon into a greased loaf pan, 9 x 5 x 3 inches, or 2 small pans, 5 x 3 x 2 inches, and bake for 1 hour.

154

# MR. AND MRS. JOEY ADAMS

# Thanksgiving Dinner Rolls

3 cups flour
½ tablespoon salt
¼ pound butter (1 stick)
¼ cup evaporated milk
¼ cup water
1 tablespoon sugar
2 packages active dry yeast
2 eggs, slightly beaten
margarine for muffin pans

Sift 1½ cups of the flour and the salt into a bowl. Heat butter, evaporated milk, water and sugar together until butter is melted. (If liquid is hotter than 115°F., let it cool to 105° to 115°F.) Stir in yeast; let it stand for 2 or 3 minutes, then stir to dissolve. Pour into the sifted flour, mix well, and beat until smooth. Cover, and let stand in a warm place (80° to 85°F.) for 20 minutes.

Add eggs and remaining 1½ cups flour to the yeast mixture, and beat vigorously. Knead the dough in the bowl until it is smooth and satiny. If it is too sticky to handle, add a little more flour. Cover dough and let it rise for about 1 hour, until doubled in bulk.

Knead down the risen dough and divide into 20 to 24 pieces. Form into 1½-inch balls and place in muffin pans greased with margarine. (Margarine is better than oil for this as it keeps the rolls from sliding around.) Let rolls stand at room temperature for about 2 hours, until doubled in size. Meanwhile preheat oven to 425°F. Bake the rolls for 10 to 15 minutes, until golden brown. Makes 20 to 24 rolls.

## DEBBIE REYNOLDS

# Hush Puppies

1 ½ cups white cornmeal
½ cup sifted flour
1 tablespoon sugar
2 teaspoons baking powder
½ teaspoon salt
1 onion, peeled and minced
1 egg, beaten
¾ cup milk
oil for deep-frying

Mix dry ingredients together. Add onion and egg, then the milk. Stir all together lightly. Scoop up portions of the batter with a small spoon, and drop into oil heated to 375°F. on a frying thermometer. Fry until golden, and serve hot, hot, hot! Makes about 4 servings.

## MIKE ARRABIA

# English Muffins

2 packages active dry yeast
½ cup warm water (105° to 115°F.)
1 cup milk
2 tablespoons sugar
2½ teaspoons salt
½ cup melted shortening
½ cup cool water
6 cups flour
cornmeal or hominy grits

Dissolve yeast in the warm water. Scald milk and stir in sugar, salt and shortening until sugar is dissolved. Add cool water to milk mixture; when it is cooled to lukewarm, add dissolved yeast and mix in the flour. Knead the dough for about 10 minutes, to make a smooth elastic dough. Put dough in a greased bowl, turn to grease dough on all sides, and cover. Let the dough rise for about 1 hour, until doubled in bulk.

Punch down dough, roll out to a sheet ¾ inch thick, and cut into 20 muffins. Sprinkle cornmeal or grits on 2 ungreased baking sheets, and place 10 muffins on each one. Sprinkle tops of muffins with more cornmeal or grits. Cover, and let muffins rise until doubled, about 1 hour.

Preheat oven to 350°F. Bake muffins for 10 minutes on each side, then reduce oven heat to 300°F. and bake for 20 minutes longer, until cooked through.

Break or tear muffins open, and serve hot with butter or jam. Or toast them before serving. Makes 20 muffins.

157

## THE HONORABLE
## FELISA RINCON DE GAUTIER

# Raisin Biscuits

2 cups sifted all-purpose flour
1 tablespoon double-acting baking powder
1 teaspoon salt
1 cup nonfat dry milk
¼ pound butter or margarine (1 stick)
½ cup firmly packed brown sugar
¾ cup cold water
¾ cup light or dark seedless raisins

Preheat oven to 400°F. Lightly grease 12 depressions in a muffin pan. Sift together flour, baking powder, salt and dry milk. Cut butter or margarine into dry ingredients until mixture is like coarse cornmeal. Dissolve brown sugar in cold water; stir the mixture and the raisins into the other ingredients. Mix to a smooth dough. Spoon ½ cup of the batter into each depression. Bake in the preheated oven for 20 to 25 minutes, until biscuits are golden brown and pull away from the muffin cups. Remove from the pan at once. Serve warm or cold, with butter and jelly. Makes 12 large biscuits.

## ROSE MORGAN

# Honey Buns

½ cup milk
7 tablespoons butter or margarine, melted
¼ cup granulated sugar
½ teaspoon salt
½ cup warm water (105° to 115°F.)
2 packages active dry yeast
1 egg
3½ cups unsifted flour
1 cup chopped unsalted peanuts
1 cup firmly packed brown sugar
⅔ cup honey
additional melted butter or margarine

Scald milk and stir in 4 tablespoons of the butter, the granulated sugar and the salt; cool to lukewarm. Pour warm water into a large bowl and sprinkle in the yeast; stir until yeast is dissolved. Add milk mixture, the egg and 2 cups of the flour; beat until smooth. Stir in enough additional flour to make a soft dough. Turn dough out on a lightly floured board and knead for 10 minutes, until dough is smooth and elastic. Place dough in a greased bowl and turn to grease all sides. Cover bowl and let dough rise in a warm draft-free place, 80° to 85°F., until doubled in bulk, about 45 minutes.

While dough rises, combine half of peanuts, half of brown sugar, the honey and remaining melted butter, and blend well. Divide mixture among 24 greased muffin cups.

When dough is doubled, punch down, turn out on a lightly floured board, and divide into halves. Roll out one half to a rectangle 12 x 9 inches. Brush dough with melted butter. Combine remaining peanuts and brown sugar, and sprinkle half over the dough. Roll up dough tightly from a 12-inch side, as if rolling a jelly roll, and seal edges firmly. Cut the roll into 12 pieces and place each one, cut side up, in a muffin cup. Prepare the rest of the dough and peanut mixture in the same way, and fill remaining muffin cups. Cover both pans of buns and again let them rise in a warm draft-free place until doubled in bulk, about 40 minutes.

Preheat oven to 375°F. Bake the buns for 15 to 20 minutes, or until done to your taste. Turn out of pans immediately. Makes 24 buns.

# 10

## DESSERTS

# MRS. KURT WALDHEIM

# Soufflé Rothschild

3 ½ ounces plus 2 teaspoons powdered
    sugar
2 ounces flour
7 eggs, separated
1 ½ cups milk
sweet butter for pans
flour for pans
1 cup apricot jam, approximately
1 cup heavy cream

Put 3 ½ ounces sugar, the flour, egg yolks and milk in the top part of a large double boiler over boiling water, and beat until creamy. Remove from heat, take top pan from boiling water, and let the mixture cool, stirring occasionally until cold. Beat egg whites until stiff. Fold egg whites into the first mixture. Butter and dust with flour 2 springform pans 8 ½ inches in diameter and 1 ½ inches high. Spoon soufflé batter evenly into the pans. They can rest in the refrigerator for 1 ½ to 2 hours before baking.

Preheat oven to 300°F. Put the pans of batter into oven and at once reduce temperature to 275°F. Bake the soufflés for about 25 minutes; they should not become very colored, but neither should they remain creamy inside. Unmold the soufflés and place one on a round silver plate. Add a few drops of boiling water to the jam and mix until the texture is smooth and creamy. With a knife spread the jam over the first soufflé, then place the second soufflé on top.

Beat the cream with 2 teaspoons sugar until stiff. Just before serving the hot soufflé, spoon whipped cream on top. It will melt and run down the soufflé very quickly. Makes 8 servings.

THE HONORABLE
HUGH CAREY

# Snow Pudding
# with
# Custard Sauce

¾ cup fresh lemon juice
1 ½ cups granulated sugar
1 cup hot water
2 packages unflavored gelatin
½ cup cold water
6 egg whites
1 teaspoon vanilla extract
1 teaspoon almond extract

¼ teaspoon cream of tartar
butter for mold

Mix lemon juice, ½ cup of the sugar and the hot water in a large saucepan. Bring to a boil and simmer until sugar is dissolved. Sprinkle gelatin on cold water to soften. Stir into the lemon-juice mixture, stir to dissolve gelatin, and let mixture cool. Beat egg whites with vanilla and almond extracts and cream of tartar until very thick. Beat in remaining 1 cup sugar until very stiff. Fold into the first mixture until smooth. Pour into a buttered 6-cup mold. Chill. Makes 6 servings.

## Custard Sauce

1 ½ cups half and half or light cream
6 egg yolks
½ cup sugar
1 teaspoon vanilla extract
2 teaspoons lemon extract

Heat half and half in the top part of a double boiler, over steaming water, until just at the boiling point. Add egg yolks and sugar, stirring all the while, and continue to stir until the custard coats the spoon. Add vanilla and lemon extracts, stir well, then put through a strainer into a cold sauce dish. Makes about 4 cups.

## MRS. HERBERT LEHMAN

# Chocolate Mousse

1 pound dark sweet chocolate
2 ounces unsweetened chocolate
7 tablespoons prepared strong coffee
2 tablespoons kirsch or rum
5 eggs, separated
2 ounces unsalted butter
1 cup heavy cream
butter for mold
2 dozen ladyfingers
whipped cream, shredded chocolate

Cut up sweet and unsweetened chocolate and place in a large heavy pot over low heat. Add coffee and stir until chocolate is dissolved. Add kirsch or rum and remove from heat. Add the egg yolks, one at a time, beating well with a whisk after each addition. Add the butter, bit by bit. Let the chocolate mixture cool. Pour the cream into a bowl set in a pan of crushed ice, and beat until cream is doubled and thick. Add cream gradually to chocolate mixture. Beat egg whites until stiff but not dry, and gently fold into the mousse. Lightly butter a 9-inch charlotte mold, and line it with split ladyfingers. Spoon in the mousse, cover the mold, and chill in the freezer overnight.

Remove mold to room temperature and let it warm slightly. Wrap a hot towel around the mold, and slide a thin-bladed knife between mold and mousse to loosen it all around. Place a flat serving dish upside down on the mold, hold both tightly together, and turn over to release the mousse. Decorate with more whipped cream and shredded chocolate. Makes 10 servings.

If you have a 9-inch springform pan, do not use a hot towel; simply reverse the pan on the serving plate and carefully release the outer rim of the springform.

# JOYCE D. BROTHERS

## Floating Island

3 or 4 egg yolks
7 tablespoons sugar
¼ teaspoon salt
2 cups milk
1 ½ teaspoons vanilla extract
3 egg whites

Beat egg yolks lightly, then add 4 tablespoons of the sugar and ⅛ teaspoon salt. Scald the milk and slowly stir it into the egg yolks. Turn custard into a saucepan over very low heat or into the top part of a double boiler over boiling water. Cook, stirring constantly, until the custard begins to thicken; do not let it boil. Strain and cool the custard. Add 1 teaspoon vanilla to the custard, stir, then pour the custard into a shallow 6-cup baking dish.

Whip egg whites with ⅛ teaspoon salt until stiff. Then very slowly, whipping constantly, add in remaining 3 tablespoons sugar and remaining ½ teaspoon vanilla, or instead of vanilla use a few drops of almond extract. Heap the meringue on the custard. Place the baking dish in a preheated 500°F. oven for 2 minutes, or slide under a broiler, until the tips of the meringue are brown. Makes 6 servings.

# MRS. HELEN HINES

## Lemon Sponge Pie

2 ounces butter, softened
1 cup sugar
3 tablespoons flour
3 eggs, separated

6 tablespoons fresh lemon juice
1 teaspoon grated lemon rind
2 cups milk

Preheat oven to 425°F. In a mixing bowl cream the butter, add sugar and flour gradually, and mix well. Add egg yolks and beat well. Add lemon juice and rind, then slowly beat in the milk. Beat egg whites until stiff, then gently fold into the lemon mixture. Spoon into a 9-inch pie pan. (There is no piecrust.) Bake in the preheated oven for 15 minutes. Reduce temperature to 325°F. and bake for 30 minutes longer. Makes 6 servings.

ED SULLIVAN

# My Mother's Bread Pudding

2 cups fine dry bread crumbs
3 cups milk
3 eggs, separated
½ cup sugar
1 teaspoon vanilla extract
grated nutmeg
⅔ cup currant jelly, approximately

Preheat oven to 350°F. Pour the bread crumbs into an ungreased 1½-quart casserole. Scald the milk and add to crumbs. Beat the egg yolks and 1 egg white just until mixed. Add eggs to crumbs along with ¼ cup sugar and the vanilla. Sprinkle with nutmeg. Set the casserole in a pan containing 1 inch of hot water. Bake for 1¼ hours, until a silver knife inserted 1 inch from the edge comes out clean.

Remove pudding from oven and spoon a thin layer of currant jelly over the top. Beat remaining 2 egg whites until thick, then continue to beat while adding remaining ¼ cup sugar, 1 tablespoon at a time. Spoon the meringue over the pudding and return to the oven. Bake for about 15 minutes, until meringue is well browned. Cool the pudding for 20 to 30 minutes before serving. Makes 8 to 10 servings.

## MRS. ELINOR SEARLE WHITNEY McCOLLUM

# Frozen Orange Marshmallow Ice

Cover the bottom of an ice-cube tray, with dividers removed, with marshmallows. Pour in enough strained hot (not boiled) orange juice to cover marshmallows. Separate them a little with a fork so they absorb some of the hot juice. If tray is deep enough, add a second layer of marshmallows and more juice. Let stand until cool, then put in freezer. When the mixture starts to become solid, mix gently with a fork, pushing marshmallows down in the tray. Cut into sections and serve by itself or with cold orange slices.

## CAROL BURNETT

# Ginger
# Ice Cream

½ gallon vanilla ice cream
1 cup chopped candied gingerroot
1 tablespoon liquid ginger

Remove ice cream from the carton, put it into a large bowl, and let it soften. When it reaches this stage, add the chopped gingerroot and liquid ginger. (Liquid ginger is obtained by pressing fresh gingerroot through a garlic press.) Mix well. Return to the ice-cream carton, or transfer to plastic containers with tight-fitting covers, and store in the freezer. Allow a week for the ginger flavor to permeate the cream thoroughly. Makes 8 servings.

# HARRY RICHMAN

# Fruta Almina

4 to 6 medium-ripe nice pears
1 cup water
½ cup white corn syrup
dash of salt
½ teaspoon vanilla extract
6 tablespoons sugar
3 egg yolks
¾ teaspoon cornstarch
⅔ cup milk
grated rind of 1 orange

2 tablespoons heavy cream
juice of ½ orange
¼ to ⅓ cup heavy cream, whipped
 (optional)
grated nutmeg

Peel the pears, cut into halves, and core them. Gently place in a saucepan and add the cup of water, the corn syrup, dash of salt, the vanilla and 3 tablespoons of the sugar. Bring to a simmer and poach for about 5 minutes, or until the pears are tender. Set pears aside to cool.

Place egg yolks with remaining 3 tablespoons sugar and the cornstarch in a saucepan over low heat, or in the top part of a double boiler over steaming water. Beat until well blended. Add the milk little by little, stirring all the while, then add orange rind. Continue to cook and stir until custard is thickened. Remove sauce from heat and allow it to cool. Add 2 tablespoons cream and the orange juice. To make the sauce thicker, fold whipped cream into the cold sauce.

Remove poached pears from syrup and arrange in a serving dish. Spoon the chilled creamy sauce over pears and sprinkle with nutmeg. Makes 8 to 12 servings.

# DINA MERRILL

## Fruit Cup with Wine

2 large oranges
1 large red apple
1 ripe Anjou pear
⅓ cup pitted dates
1 large ripe banana
¾ cup Tokay grapes
1 pomegranate
¼ cup Rhine wine
6 sprigs of fresh mint

Peel and section orange. Core and cut up apple and pear. Sliver dates. Peel banana and cut into diagonal slices. Halve the grapes and remove seeds. Peel pomegranate and separate seeds. In a large bowl combine the fruits, pomegranate seeds and wine; mix well. Cover and refrigerate until serving time. Before serving toss again to mix well. Spoon fruits and liquid into sherbet dishes and top each with a sprig of mint. Makes 6 servings.

*Dina Merrill adds, "My favorite new dessert is a pineapple, quartered lengthwise. Pour Grand Marnier over it, ignite the liqueur, and serve it flambé."*

# MRS. DWIGHT D. EISENHOWER

# Frosted
# Mint Delight

2 cans (1 pound each) crushed pineapple
1 package unflavored gelatin
¾ cup mint-flavored apple jelly
2 cups heavy cream
2 teaspoons confectioners' sugar

Open pineapple and pour off 1 cup of the juice. Sprinkle gelatin over the juice to soften. Melt the jelly over low heat and mix the pineapple into it. Stir gelatin mixture into pineapple and stir until gelatin is dissolved. Cool. Whip the cream, sweeten it with the sugar, and fold it into the pineapple mixture. Put in the freezer until firm but not frozen solid. Makes 10 or 12 servings.

MME MIMI LEEUWENBERG

# Yogurt Dessert

Arrange a bowl or platter of fresh fruits—green, red and blue grapes, orange and grapefruit sections, peach slices, banana quarters, strawberries. Beat 1 cup of plain yogurt with ½ cup whipped cream and 3 tablespoons sugar. Spoon over the fruits, and top with thawed frozen raspberries.

# 11

---

## CAKES AND PIES

PRESIDENT AND
MRS. LYNDON B. JOHNSON

# Lemon Cake with Lemon Icing

1¼ cups sugar
6 ounces butter
8 egg yolks
2½ cups sifted cake flour
1 tablespoon baking powder
¼ teaspoon salt
¾ cup milk
1 teaspoon vanilla extract
1 teaspoon fresh lemon juice
1 teaspoon grated lemon rind
butter for pans

Preheat oven to 375°F. Sift the sugar. Beat butter in a large bowl until soft, then gradually add the sugar. Blend until the mixture is very light and creamy. Beat egg yolks in a separate bowl until very light and lemon-colored, then blend them into the butter mixture. Sift cake flour with baking powder and salt 3 times. Add dry ingredients to the butter mixture, one third at a time, alternately with the milk, ¼ cup at a time. Beat the batter thoroughly after each addition. Add vanilla, lemon juice and rind, and beat the batter for 2 minutes. Butter two 9-inch layer-cake pans, and divide the batter between them. Bake in the preheated oven for about 20 minutes. Cool layers, then spread with lemon icing (recipe follows) and fit the layers together.

## Lemon Icing

2 cups confectioners' sugar
2 ounces butter, softened
grated rind and juice of 1 lemon
1 or more teaspoons cream

Blend sugar and butter well. Beat in lemon rind and juice, then add just enough cream to give the right texture to the icing. Makes enough icing for 2 layers.

174

# PRESIDENT
# RICHARD M. NIXON

# Cheesecake

1 pound cream cheese
1 pound creamed cottage cheese
1½ cups sugar
4 eggs, slightly beaten
3 tablespoons cornstarch
3 tablespoons flour
1½ tablespoons fresh lemon juice
1 teaspoon grated lemon rind
1 teaspoon vanilla extract

¼ pound butter (1 stick), melted
2 cups dairy sour cream

Preheat oven to 325°F. Butter a 9-inch springform pan. In the large bowl of an electric mixer, beat cream cheese with cottage cheese at high speed until they are well combined. Gradually beat in sugar, then eggs. At low speed beat in cornstarch, flour, lemon juice and rind, and vanilla. Add melted butter and sour cream and beat just until mixture is smooth. Pour into the prepared pan, and bake in the preheated oven for 1 hour and 10 minutes, or until firm around the edges. Turn off the oven, and let the pan remain in the oven for 2 hours.

Remove cake from oven and let it cool for 2 hours, then refrigerate it for 3 hours, or until it is well chilled. Run a spatula around the edge of the cake, then release the rim of the springform. Leave the cake on the pan bottom and slide it onto a large serving plate.

175

## MRS. BARRY GOLDWATER

# Favorite
# Chocolate Cake

2 cups all-purpose flour
2 cups sugar
¼ pound margarine (1 stick), softened
1 teaspoon salt
¾ tablespoon baking soda
3 heaping tablespoons cocoa powder
1 ½ cups milk

¾ teaspoon baking powder
3 eggs, unbeaten
1 teaspoon vanilla extract
red food coloring (optional)

Preheat oven to 350°F. Butter two 9-inch layer-cake pans, line with paper, and butter the paper. Mix in a large bowl the flour, sugar, margarine, salt, baking soda, cocoa powder and 1 cup of the milk. Blend by hand for 2 minutes. Stir in the baking powder, then add remaining milk, the eggs and vanilla. Blend by hand for another 2 minutes. Add a little red food coloring, if you like, for a nice color. Pour batter into the prepared pans and bake in the preheated oven for 30 to 35 minutes. Let cakes cool, then put together with filling or frosting as you like.

# Red Devil's-Food Cake

*Evelyn Roberts says, "My grandchildren love this cake!"*

2 cups sugar
½ cup shortening or margarine
2 eggs, beaten
½ cup buttermilk
pinch of salt
1¼ teaspoons baking soda

2 cups flour
4 tablespoons cocoa powder
1 cup boiling water
1 teaspoon vanilla extract

Preheat oven to 325°F. Grease two 8-inch layer-cake pans or a single oblong pan 13 x 9 inches. Cream sugar and shortening; add eggs and beat well. Add buttermilk, salt and baking soda; mix. Add flour and cocoa, then boiling water, then vanilla, mixing well after each addition. Batter will be thin. Pour into the prepared pans and bake in the preheated oven for 35 to 45 minutes. Let cake cool, then ice.

## Uncooked Icing

⅔ cup white corn syrup
1 egg white
1 teaspoon vanilla extract
red food coloring (optional)

With the mixer at high speed, beat corn syrup and egg white until the mixture reaches spreading consistency. Add vanilla. Add red coloring if you want to make the icing pink.

## LOTTE LENYA

# Viennese Vacherin

12 egg whites
⅛ teaspoon salt
1 teaspoon cream of tartar
3 cups fine sugar
4 cups heavy cream
2½ tablespoons confectioners' sugar
1 teaspoon vanilla extract
1 quart strawberries

Preheat oven to 200°F. Drop 8 egg whites into a large mixer bowl, and add half of the salt. With an electric mixer, beat until frothy. Add half of the cream of tartar, and continue to beat. Add 1½ cups of the fine sugar, spooning it in 1 tablespoon at a time, and continuing to beat. When mixture is smooth and glossy, fold in ¼ cup more fine sugar, and beat until sugar is no longer grainy. Transfer meringue to a large piping bag fitted with a No. 8 plain tube.

Moisten 5 baking sheets and cover with heavy brown paper. On each one mark off an 8-inch circle. Beginning in the center of one circle, pipe out meringue in a snail pattern, going around and around until the circle is filled; this will be the bottom of the cake. On the next 3 circles pipe meringue only around the outside edge, making a ring 2 layers high; these will be the sides of the cake. For the last circle, change the tube to a No. 6 star tube. With this pipe a single thick layer around the edge to make a ring, then fill the center with a crisscrossed lattice pattern of meringue. Bake all 5 circles in the preheated oven for 2½ hours, until they are crisp but not browned. When they are cool and you are sure they are dry, carefully remove the brown paper.

Drop remaining 4 egg whites into the mixer bowl, and add remaining salt; beat until frothy. Add remaining cream of tartar and beat until peaks form. Add 1 cup of the fine sugar, 1 tablespoon at a time, and beat until smooth and glossy. Fold in remaining ¼ cup fine sugar and beat until sugar is no longer grainy.

Again preheat oven, this time to 150°F. Put the solid meringue circle on a silver serving plate. Dab uncooked meringue around the edges, and put the first baked ring in place. Dab this with uncooked meringue and add the second ring, then repeat with the third ring. If any of the baked meringue layers breaks, use unbaked meringue to glue it together again. With a spatula spread unbaked meringue all around the outside of the shell, like a frosting, to make a smooth surface. Put remaining unbaked meringue in a piping bag fitted with a No. 6 star tube. Decorate the sides and base of the shell. Bake again for 2 hours.

Whip the cream with the confectioners' sugar and vanilla. Wash and stem strawberries, and roll in paper towels to dry. Reserve a few of the most perfect berries for garnish, and slice the rest. Combine berries and whipped cream and gently fill the meringue shell. Place the latticed meringue layer on top and decorate with any remaining cream and the reserved whole berries. Makes 8 servings.

## MADAME
## HELENA RUBENSTEIN

# Coconut
# Fudge Cake

### Coconut-Fudge Filling

¼ cup sugar
1 teaspoon vanilla extract
8 ounces cream cheese
1 egg
½ cup flaked coconut
6 ounces chocolate chips (1 cup)

Make the filling first. Combine sugar, vanilla, cream cheese and egg in a small bowl and mix until smooth. Stir in coconut and chocolate chips. Set aside.

### Cake Batter

2 cups sugar
1 cup cooking oil
2 eggs
3 cups self-rising flour
¾ cup unsweetened cocoa powder
1 teaspoon baking soda
1 cup sour milk, or 1 cup fresh milk mixed
    with 2 tablespoons lemon juice
1 teaspoon vanilla extract
½ cup chopped pecans

Grease and flour a 10-inch tube pan. Preheat oven to 350°F. In a large mixer bowl combine sugar, oil and eggs. Beat at high speed for 1 minute. Add flour, cocoa, baking soda, sour milk and vanilla. Beat at medium speed for 3 minutes; scrape the bowl. Stir in pecans by hand.

    Spoon two thirds of cake batter into the prepared tube pan. Spread the filling over the batter. Spoon in remaining batter. Bake for 70 to 75 minutes, or up to 25 minutes longer, until cake is baked. Cool the cake upright for 15 minutes, then remove from the pan. Cool completely, then drizzle with glaze (recipe follows).

## Glaze

1 cup powdered sugar
3 tablespoons unsweetened cocoa powder
2 tablespoons butter or margarine
2 teaspoons vanilla extract
1 to 3 tablespoons hot water

Mix sugar, cocoa, butter and vanilla. Add hot water, 1 tablespoon at a time, adding only enough to make a smooth glaze.

# JOAN CRAWFORD

# Angel-Food Cake

1 cup cake flour
⅞ cup plus ¾ cup sugar
1 ½ cups egg whites (about 12 egg whites)
½ tablespoon cream of tartar
½ tablespoon vanilla extract
¼ teaspoon almond extract
¼ teaspoon salt

Preheat oven to 350°F. Sift cake flour and ⅞ cup sugar together 3 times. Put egg whites, cream of tartar, flavorings and salt in a large bowl and beat with a wire whisk until foamy. Add remaining ¾ cup sugar, 2 tablespoons at a time, and continue beating until the meringue holds stiff peaks. Gradually sift flour mixture over the meringue and fold in gently until flour disappears. Spoon the batter into an ungreased 10-inch tube pan, and gently cut through the batter with a knife. Bake in the preheated oven for 1 hour. Invert the pan over a funnel until cake is cool.

# BELLA ABZUG

# Fabulous Cheesecake

graham-cracker crust
1½ pounds pot cheese
¼ pound cream cheese
¼ pound farmer cheese
6 eggs, separated
1 teaspoon vanilla extract
2 tablespoons cornstarch
2 ounces butter, melted
½ cup dairy sour cream
1 cup sugar

Butter the sides and base of a 9-inch springform pan, and press the graham-cracker crust on the base only. Preheat oven to 300°F. Press the cheeses twice through a colander into a large bowl, using the bottom of a heavy glass as a pusher. Add egg yolks, vanilla, cornstarch, butter, sour cream and sugar to cheese and mix well. Beat egg whites until stiff. Gently fold them into the cheese mixture. Spoon batter into the prepared pan. Bake in the preheated oven for 1 hour, then with the oven door closed let the cake cool in the oven. Don't open the door or look in!

## MR. AND MRS. ROBERT KENNEDY

# Chocolate Roll

6 tablespoons flour
6 tablespoons cocoa powder
½ teaspoon baking powder
¼ teaspoon salt
4 eggs, separated
¾ cup sugar
1 teaspoon vanilla extract
powdered sugar or cocoa powder
whipped cream

Oil a jelly-roll pan, 10 x 15 inches, line with wax paper, and oil the paper. Preheat oven to 400°F. Sift flour, cocoa, baking powder and salt together. Beat egg yolks with sugar until sugar is no longer grainy. Gently add sifted ingredients and mix. Beat egg whites until stiff, then fold them and vanilla into the batter. Spoon batter into the prepared pan, smoothing it even with a spatula. Bake in the preheated oven for 12 minutes.

While cake bakes, spread out another sheet of wax paper and dust it with powdered sugar or cocoa. Turn the baked cake out on the prepared paper, peel off the paper on the bottom, and roll up the cake in the sugared wax paper. Cool.

When cake is cool, unroll, spread with whipped cream, and roll up, without the wax paper this time. Wrap, and store in the freezer until shortly before serving time.

MRS. GERALD R. FORD

# Strawberry Blitz Torte

1 cup sifted cake flour
1 teaspoon baking powder
¾ teaspoon salt
½ cup shortening
1 ½ cups sugar
4 eggs, separated
3 tablespoons milk
1 ½ teaspoons vanilla extract
½ teaspoon cream of tartar
Strawberry Filling (recipe follows)

Grease two 8-inch layer-cake pans. Preheat oven to 350°F. Sift flour, baking powder and ¼ teaspoon of the salt together 3 times. Cream shortening; add ½ cup of the sugar slowly, and cream together until light and fluffy. Beat egg yolks until thick and add to creamed mixture. Stir in milk and 1 teaspoon of the vanilla. Add sifted dry ingredients and beat until batter is smooth. Spread batter into the prepared pans.

Make a meringue: Beat egg whites, remaining ½ teaspoon salt and the cream of tartar until soft peaks form when beater is lifted. Add remaining 1 cup sugar, 2 tablespoons at a time, beating thoroughly after each addition. Add remaining ½ teaspoon vanilla. Spread half of meringue over each pan of batter. Bake the layers in the preheated oven for about 35 minutes.

Remove from oven, loosen sides of layers from the pans, and remove the layers to wire racks, keeping the meringue on top. When cool, spread strawberry filling on one layer and top with the second layer.

## Strawberry Filling

½ cup heavy cream
2 tablespoons confectioners' sugar
1 cup sliced hulled strawberries

Whip cream with sugar until stiff. Fold in strawberries. Spread on bottom torte layer.

185

# NELSON A. ROCKEFELLER

## New York State Flat Apple Pie

4 cups flour
½ pound butter (2 sticks)
½ pound margarine (2 sticks)
6 tablespoons ice water
8 apples
1 cup sugar
1 tablespoon ground cinnamon
lemon juice
½ cup New York State maple syrup

Put flour, butter and margarine on a marble slab (or wooden countertop) and cut butter and margarine with a knife, mixing it into the flour, until the mixture is like cornmeal. Transfer to a bowl and add ice water. Handle the dough only just enough so that it stays together. Roll out to 1-inch thickness, then refrigerate for 20 minutes. Roll out chilled dough once more, this time to a sheet ⅛ inch thick. Fit the dough into a flat pan or baking sheet 15 x 10 inches.

Preheat oven to 450°F. Peel and core apples, and cut each one into 6 sections. Arrange the pieces in a single layer on the dough. Sprinkle with the sugar and cinnamon, and also with a little lemon juice. Bake in the preheated oven for 20 minutes, then reduce heat to 350°F. and bake for 30 minutes longer. Remove pie from oven and sprinkle with the maple syrup. Serve while still warm, with a generous slice of sharp cheese. Makes about 15 pieces, 3 inches square.

# ART LINKLETTER

# Strawberry Cheese Pie

⅓ pound honey graham crackers
1¼ cups plus 2 tablespoons sugar
¼ pound butter (1 stick), softened
1 pound and 6 ounces cream cheese
5 extra large eggs
juice of 1 lemon
2 cups dairy sour cream
1 teaspoon vanilla extract
1 quart fresh strawberries

Crush graham crackers with a rolling pin until they are fine crumbs. Stir in ¼ cup of the sugar and the softened butter. Mix well, then press into the bottom and up the sides of a deep 10-inch pie plate.

Preheat oven to 350°F. Beat the cream cheese with 1 cup sugar until smooth. Add the eggs, one at a time, beating well after each addition. Add lemon juice. Pour cheese filling into the prepared crumb crust. Bake in the preheated oven for about 50 minutes, until done. Let cool for about 15 minutes.

Mix sour cream with vanilla and remaining 2 tablespoons sugar. Spread on top of the pie and return it to the oven for 10 minutes.

Let pie cool. Store it in the refrigerator; the flavor will be improved on the second day. Wash and hull strawberries, and let them dry well. Spread them on top of the pie. Makes 12 servings.

BOB HOPE

# Lemon Meringue Pie

3 tablespoons cornstarch
1 cup plus 2½ tablespoons sugar
1 cup boiling water
4 egg yolks
2 tablespoons butter
grated rind of 1 lemon
¼ cup fresh lemon juice
pinch of salt
1 baked pastry shell, 9 inches
3 egg whites

Mix cornstarch into 1 cup of the sugar in a large saucepan. Add the boiling water slowly, stirring constantly, until mixture is thick and smooth. Beat egg yolks lightly and stir into sugar mixture, stirring constantly. Add butter, lemon rind, lemon juice and salt. Cook for 2 or 3 minutes, until smooth and translucent. Spoon into the baked pastry shell.

Make a meringue: Beat the egg whites until stiff, then continue to beat while adding remaining 2½ tablespoons sugar, little by little, until meringue is very thick and shiny. Cover the lemon pie with the meringue, making sure it touches the pie crust all around. Bake in a preheated 300°F. oven for about 15 minutes, until meringue is light brown. Makes 6 servings.

# ABIGAIL VANBUREN

## Abby's Pecan Pie

*"This pie is a 'specialty of the house' at the Phoenix Hotel in Lexington, Kentucky. I begged this off the pastry chef to share with you."*

1 cup white corn syrup
1 cup dark brown sugar
⅓ teaspoon salt
⅓ cup melted butter
1 teaspoon vanilla extract
3 whole eggs
1 heaping cup shelled pecans
pastry for 1-crust, 9-inch pie, unbaked

Preheat oven to 350°F. Mix corn syrup, brown sugar, salt, melted butter and vanilla. Beat eggs slightly and mix in. Pour into the pastry-lined pie pan. Sprinkle pecans over the top. Bake for about 45 minutes. Makes 8 servings.

# MRS. ELEANOR ROOSEVELT

# Nesselrode Pie with Infallible Piecrust

## Infallible Piecrust

2 cups flour
1 teaspoon salt
½ cup vegetable shortening
ice water
1 or 2 tablespoons butter

Sift the flour 3 times, the third time with the salt. With a pastry blender or 2 silver knives, cut shortening into flour until the mixture looks crumbly, like coarse cornmeal. Mix in ice water, 1 tablespoon at a time, until you have a stiff dough. Roll out the dough and spread it with part of the butter. Fold over the dough and butter again. Continue buttering and folding until 1 tablespoon has been used. A second tablespoon will make it even better.

Preheat oven to 400°F. Roll out half of the pastry to a thin sheet, and fit it into a 9-inch pie dish. (Remaining pastry can be wrapped and refrigerated for another pie.) Line the dough with foil and fill with weights (dried beans, etc.). Bake in the preheated oven for 10 minutes. Remove weights and foil, and bake for another 5 to 10 minutes, until pastry is cooked and golden in color. Let it cool.

## Nesselrode Pie

4 eggs, separated
1 cup sugar
¼ teaspoon salt
2 cups milk
1 envelope unflavored gelatin
½ cup heavy cream
½ teaspoon rum
1 tablespoon minced candied cherries
½ cup semisweet chocolate chips, grated

Drop egg yolks into the top part of a large double boiler. Beat lightly, then add ½ cup of the sugar and the salt. Heat 1¾ cups of the milk and slowly pour it into the

190

egg-yolk mixture. Pour hot water into the bottom part of the double boiler, place over moderate heat, and set the top pan in place. Cook the custard, stirring constantly, until it coats a metal spoon. Remove from hot water and set aside.

Pour remaining ¼ cup cold milk into a large bowl, and sprinkle gelatin over it to soften. Pour in the hot custard and stir until gelatin is dissolved. Add cream and rum (more rum can be added to taste). Chill the custard until it begins to thicken.

Beat egg whites until thick, then add remaining ½ cup sugar, little by little, and continue to beat until stiff peaks form when beater is lifted. Fold in the cherries. Fold meringue into the cooled custard. Spoon Nesselrode filling in the cooled baked pie shell and chill until firm. Sprinkle grated chocolate chips over the top. Makes 6 servings.

# 12

---

## AFTER DINNER

## MRS. NAT M. GREENBLATT

# Café Brûlot

8 ounces Cognac
40 whole cloves
2 cinnamon sticks, broken into pieces
very thin peel of 1 lemon
very thin peel of 1 orange
32 lumps of sugar
6 cups prepared strong coffee, piping hot

Pour Cognac into a *brûlot* bowl over an alcohol burner. (If you do not have such a bowl, use a chafing dish or a metal bowl set over a fondue burner.) Add spices, fruit peels and sugar. Ignite the alcohol in the burner underneath. Stir the contents of the bowl over heat until it ignites. Let it burn for only a few minutes, so that it may not burn up all the alcohol in the Cognac. Slowly pour the coffee into the bowl, letting the flames last so that it is as dramatic as can be. Ladle coffee into demitasse cups. Makes enough for about 20 demitasse servings.
*Note:* The amount of sugar can be varied to taste. This amount (2 lumps per cup of coffee, plus 20 more) may seem excessive, but *café brûlot* should taste like a very rich fruitcake.

BING CROSBY

# Hello Dolly
# Cookies

¼ pound margarine (1 stick)
1 cup graham-cracker crumbs
1 cup shredded coconut
1 cup chopped walnuts
8 ounces semisweet chocolate chips
1 can (14 ounces) condensed milk

Preheat oven to 350°F. Melt margarine in a flat pan 9 x 12 inches. Pour graham-cracker crumbs over margarine and spread evenly over pan. Add coconut, then nuts, then chocolate chips, each time spreading the new ingredient evenly over the one beneath. Pour condensed milk over the whole works. Bake in the preheated oven for 30 minutes. Let cool completely, then cut into squares. Makes about 24 cookies.

# DAVID HARTMAN

# Thumbprint Cookies

¼ pound butter (1 stick)
¼ pound margarine (1 stick)
½ cup sugar
2 eggs, separated
1 teaspoon vanilla extract
2 cups sifted flour

½ teaspoon salt
¾ cup crushed nuts, approximately
¾ cup apricot or strawberry preserves, approximately

Cream butter, margarine and sugar together. Beat in egg yolks and vanilla. Stir in flour and salt. Mix well. Pat out dough on a sheet of wax paper to a sheet about ½ inch thick. Refrigerate.

Preheat oven to 375°F. Beat egg whites until foamy. Make small circular patties from the dough. Dip each one into egg white, then into crushed nuts. Place cookies on baking sheets and bake in the preheated oven for 5 minutes. Remove from oven. With a thumb, press into the center of each cookie to make a depression. Fill the depressions with fruit preserves. Return to oven and bake for 10 minutes longer. Makes about 3 dozen cookies.

Apricot preserve is great for Christmastime. You've got a yellow center, naturally, and with a drop of food coloring you can have more variety in adding to a holiday assortment.

## J. PAUL GETTY

# Cocoa Fudge

4 cups sugar
4 teaspoons cocoa powder
1½ cups milk
2 teaspoons vanilla extract
2 ounces butter
butter for pan

Mix sugar, cocoa and milk in a large saucepan. Add as much vanilla as you like. Bring to a boil, stirring with a wooden spoon. Boil for about 15 minutes, until the mixture starts to thicken and crystallize around the edge of the pan. Remove from heat, add the butter, and beat hard with a spoon or an electric beater until thick. Pour into a buttered 8-inch-square pan, making a layer about ¾ inch thick. Leave it to set until cold. (If it does not set properly, it has not cooked long enough.) Cut into 1-inch squares before it is completely cold and hard. Makes 64 pieces.

MRS. JIMMY CARTER

# Peanut Brittle

3 cups sugar
1½ cups water
1 cup white corn syrup
3 cups shelled raw peanuts

2 tablespoons baking soda
2 ounces butter
1 teaspoon vanilla extract

Boil sugar, water and corn syrup until the syrup spins a thread (about 220°F. on a candy thermometer). Add peanuts, and stir continually until syrup turns golden brown. Remove pan from heat and add remaining ingredients; stir until butter melts. Quickly pour out on 2 cookie sheets with sides. As the mixture begins to harden around the edges, pull out until the brittle forms a thin sheet.

MARIA ADAMS BELL

# New Orleans
# Pecan Pralines

2 cups brown sugar
1 cup heavy cream
1 cup granulated sugar
1 cup water
3 cups slivered shelled pecans
butter for baking sheet

Cook brown sugar with the cream in one saucepan, granulated sugar with the water in another. Cook until both sugar mixtures are very thick. Combine sugar mixtures and add pecans; stir well. Drop mixture by tablespoons onto a well-buttered baking sheet, leaving space between pralines. Cool.

# Metric Conversion Tables

TEMPERATURES
*Fahrenheit → Celsius:*
  *subtract 32 from the F. figure, multiply by 5, then divide by 9.*
*Celsius → Fahrenheit:*
  *multiply C. figure by 9, divide by 5, then add 32.*

| °Fahrenheit | °Celsius | |
|---|---|---|
| 0 | –17.7 | |
| 32 | 0 | freezing |
| 50 | 10 | |
| 80 | 26.7 | raising yeast doughs |
| 85 | 29.4 | dissolving fresh yeast |
| 100 | 37.7 | |
| 105 | 40.5 | dissolving dry yeast |
| 150 ⎤ | 65.5 ⎤ | baking meringue |
| 200 ⎦ | 93.3 ⎦ | |
| 205 | 96.1 | poach or simmer |
| 212 | 100 | boil |
| 300 | 148.8 | |
| 325 | 162.8 | |
| 350 ⎤ | 177 ⎤ | |
| 375 | 190.5 | |
| 400 | 204.4 | bake |
| 425 | 218.3 | |
| 450 ⎦ | 232 ⎦ | |
| 500 | 260 | broil |

VOLUME MEASURES—LIQUID
*(based on milk and water)*

| | | |
|---|---|---|
| 1 teaspoon | = | 4.7 grams |
| 1 tablespoon | = | 14.3 grams |
| 2 tablespoons (1 ounce) | = | 28.35 grams |
| 4 tablespoons (¼ cup) | = | 56.7 grams |
| 8 tablespoons (½ cup) | = | 113.4 grams |
| 16 tablespoons (1 cup) | = | 226.8 grams |

VOLUME MEASURES—DRY
*(based on all-purpose flour)*

| | | |
|---|---|---|
| 1 teaspoon | = | 3 grams |
| 1 tablespoon | = | 9 grams |
| 2 tablespoons | = | 18 grams |
| 4 tablespoons (¼ cup) | = | 36 grams |
| 8 tablespoons (½ cup) | = | 72 grams |
| 16 tablespoons (1 cup) | = | 144 grams |

OUNCES TO GRAMS

*ounces → grams: multiply ounce figure by 28.3.*
*grams → ounces: multiply gram figure by .035.*

| | | |
|---|---|---|
| ½ ounce | = | 14.3 grams |
| 1 ounce | = | 28.35 grams |
| 2 ounces | = | 56.7 grams |
| 4 ounces | = | 113.4 grams |
| 8 ounces (½ pound) | = | 226.8 grams |
| 16 ounces (1 pound) | = | 453.6 grams or 0.4536 kilogram |

CUPS TO LITERS

| | | |
|---|---|---|
| 1 liquid ounce | = | 29.57 milliliters |
| .42 cup | = | 1 deciliter |
| ½ cup | = | 118.29 milliliters |
| 1 cup | = | 236.59 milliliters or .237* liter |
| 4 cups (1 quart) | = | 946.35 milliliters or .946 liter |

*\*(for convenience, .24 liter)*
*For convenience substitute 1 quart for 1 liter or vice versa.*

# Index of Contributors

Abzug, Bella Savitsky (Mrs. Martin Abzug): former U. S. Representative from New York; attorney, specialist in labor law and civil rights; New York City—*Fabulous Cheesecake*

Adams, Alease Lavallias: mother of Maria Adams Bell—*My Mother's Holiday Bread —Hallah*

Adams, Mr. and Mrs. Joey (Cindy Adams): television and radio; New York City—*Thanksgiving Dinner Rolls*

Alexander, The Honorable Fritz W., II: Justice of the Supreme Court; New York—*Roast Stuffed Goose*

Allen, Gracie (Mrs. George Burns), *see* Burns

Anderson, Marion: American singer, opera star; Presidential Medal of Freedom (1962); New York City—*Flounder Roulades*

Arrabia, Mike: New York City—*English Muffins*

Ashe, Arthur: American tennis player, many championships, USTA and Wimbledon; New York City—*Virginia Fried Chicken with Peas and Rice*

Bailey, Pearl: American entertainer and Broadway star; Apple Valley, Nevada—*Burgundy Meatballs*

Baker, Josephine (1906-1975): American-born Parisian singer and dancer; introduced "le jazz hot" to Paris—*Saddle of Lamb Polignac*

Ball, Lucille: American actress in films, television; "First Lady of Comedy"—*Lucy's Big Gang Special*

Barnard, Christiaan, M.D.: cardiac surgeon, The University of Cape Town, South Africa; first successful heart transplant, 1967—*Veal Scaloppini with Tomatoes*

Bassey, Shirley: Welsh-born vocalist, recording artist, concert artist—*Redfish Supreme*

Bell, Maria Adams: Founder-President, The Educational Guild for Tots to Seniors Foundation Inc.; New York City—*New Orleans Pecan Pralines*

Boone, Debby (Deborah Ann): American singer; Beverly Hills—*Vegetarian Tacos*

Braddon, Lady Violet: Woollahra, New South Wales, Australia—*Pheasant with Apples*

Bricktop, *see* de Conge

Brothers, Joyce D., Ph.D. (Mrs. Milton Brothers): psychologist, lecturer, writer, television and radio personality; Fort Lee, New Jersey—*Floating Island*

Brown, Edmund, G., Jr.: Governor of California; attorney—*Paella Amigos*

Bunche, Mrs. Ralph: widow of U. N. Under Secretary General; first black to win Nobel Peace Prize (1950); New York City—*Eggplant Provençale*

Burnett, Carol: American television comedienne, actress, singer; many awards; Los Angeles—*Ginger Ice Cream*

Burns, Mr. and Mrs. George (Gracie Allen, 1905-1964): American comedians, radio, television, films; Beverly Hills—*Egg Mousse with Seafood Salad*

Cantinflas (Mario Moreno): Mexican clown, acrobat, bullfighter and actor; Mexico City—*Cantinflas Tamale Pie*

Carey, The Honorable Hugh L.: Governor of New York; Albany, New York City—*Snow Pudding with Custard Sauce*

Carroll, Diahann: American entertainer, actress, vocalist; Los Angeles—*Brown Beef Stew*

Carter, Rosalynn S. (Mrs. Jimmy Carter): First Lady of the United States—*Peanut Brittle*

Cartland, Barbara: author, lecturer, President of the British National Association for Health—*Smoked Salmon Pâté*

Chisholm, The Honorable Shirley: U. S. Representative from New York; many awards for outstanding community service; Brooklyn—*Royal Melon Broth with Chicken Dumplings*

Claiborne, Craig: food critic and food author; food editor for *New York Times*; New York City—*Fish Soup with Croutons*

Clifford, Mrs. Clark (Marnie Clifford): Washington hostess; wife of former U. S. Secretary of Defense; Washington, D. C.—*Curry Consommé*

Clift, Montgomery (1920-1966): American stage and screen actor—*Gazpacho*

Cole, Nat "King" (1919-1965): American singer and top recording artist—*Real French Bread*

Crawford, Joan (1908-1977): actress; Academy Award 1945; one of Hollywood's most

202

glamorous stars—*Angel-Food Cake*

Crosby, Bing (1904-1977): American actor and singer; radio, television, films—*Hello Dolly Cookies*

Cummings, Joanne: international socialite; New York City—*Lobster Amandine*

Cummings, Nathan: American business executive; many international awards; New York City—*Chicken à la Cummings*

Davis, Sammy, Jr.: singer, dancer, actor, recording artist, television performer; Hollywood—*Creamed Quails*

de Conge, Madame (Bricktop): international entertainer and singer, active for six decades; Paris, Rome, New York City—*Italian Pot Roast with Noodles*

de Gautier, Felisa Rincon: former mayor of San Juan, Puerto Rico; member Democratic National Charter Committee; San Juan—*Raisin Biscuits*

Denver, John: musician, composer; pop music superstar; Aspen, Colorado—*Annie Denver's Mandarin Tossed Salad*

Desai, The Honorable Morarji R.: Prime Minister of India, following long career in fight for independence and many roles in Indian government; New Delhi—*Vegetarian Diet*

Dinkins, The Honorable David N.: City Clerk and Clerk of the Council, New York City—*Avocado Stuffed with Crab Meat*

Douglas, Mike: "The Mike Douglas Show," WCBS-TV—*Chicken Parmigiana*

Dubonnet, Mme Ruth: Paris, New York City—*Poulet Véronique*

Durante, Jimmy: American comedian in vaudeville, night clubs, films—*Chicken Noodle Soup*

Eisenhower, Dwight D. (1890-1969): President of the United States (1953-1961); General of the Army—*Meat Loaf*

Eisenhower, Mrs. Dwight D.: former First Lady of the United States; Gettysburg, Pennsylvania—*Frosted Mint Delight*

Ellington, Duke (1899-1974): American composer and musician; Presidential Medal of Freedom (1970); Légion d'Honneur (1973)—*Shrimps in Spicy Sauce*

Fields, Totie (1930-1978): American comedienne, TV and nightclubs—*Cheese Soufflé*

Fleming, Peggy (Mrs. Gregory Jenkins): superstar on ice; Olympic Gold Medal for figure skating, 1968; many awards; Los Angeles—*Crème Vichyssoise Glacée*

Ford, Gerald R.: President of the United States (1974-1977)—*Liver Deluxe*

Ford, Mrs. Gerald R. (Betty): former First Lady of the United States—*Strawberry Blitz Torte*

Ford, Henry, II: American industrialist, Chairman and Chief Executive Officer, Ford Motor Company; Grosse Pointe Farms, Michigan—*French Dressing*

Franklin, Joe: American television personality and interviewer, WOR-TV—*Broiled Mushrooms with Pâté de Foie Gras*

Galitzine, Princess Irene: dress designer; Rome—*Chicken Roll (Kournik) with Supreme Sauce*

Garland, Judy (1922-1969): American actress and singer; "The Darling of the Theatre"—*Ham Casserole with Sherry*

Getty, J. Paul (1892-1976): American oil executive and industrial oil producer—*Cocoa Fudge*

Goldman, Irving: educator, anthropologist; New York City—*Green Beans Gourmet*

Goldwater, Mrs. Barry: wife of Republican Senator from Arizona; Phoenix—*Favorite Chocolate Cake*

Goodhart, Cicely: wife of Sir Arthur Goodhart, British jurist and professor, KBE, QC; Oxford, England—*Rice Pilaff with Chicken Livers*

Goulet, Mr. and Mrs. Robert (Carol Lawrence): Canadian-American baritone and television performer; American singer and actress, stage, films, television; Beverly Hills—*Veal Scaloppini with Peppers*

Grace, Princess of Monaco: wife of Prince Rainier III of Monaco; formerly Grace Kelly, film and television actress—*Pissaladière*

Graham, Dr. and Mrs. Billy: Founder-President of Billy Graham Evangelistic Association; Montreat, North Carolina—*Home-Baked Bread*

Greenblatt, Mrs. Nat M.: New Orleans—*Café Brûlot*

Hackett, Hal: international entertainer; California, New York—*Peanut Rice (Orez Botneem)*

Harris, The Honorable Patricia Roberts: American lawyer and diplomatist; Secretary of Housing and Urban Development; Washington, D. C.—*Tropical Island Luncheon Salad*

Hartman, David: American television actor; "Good Morning America," WABC-TV; New York City—*Thumbprint Cookies*

Hayes, Helen: American actress; on stage for 60 years; also films; New York City—*Chilled Avocado Soup*

Hines, Mrs. Helen: international cosmetician,

Gaubaud de Paris, U. S. A. and France—*Lemon Sponge Pie*

Hope, Bob: American comedian, radio, television, films; Los Angeles—*Lemon Meringue Pie*

Humphrey, The Honorable Muriel (Mrs. Hubert Humphrey): widow of U. S. Senator from Minnesota and Vice-President of the United States—*Beef Soup*

Hurley, Joan: English actress; London—*Ham and Cheese Soufflé*

Jenkins, Peggy Fleming, *see* Fleming

Johnson, Lyndon Baines (1908-1973), and Mrs. Lady Bird Johnson: President of the United States (1963-1969) and First Lady—*Lemon Cake with Lemon Icing*

Jones, Ruth H. (Mrs. Raymond Jones): District Director, Treasury Department; St. Thomas, Virgin Islands—*Kallaloo with Fungi*

Kennedy, John Fitzgerald (1917-1963): President of the United States (1961-1963)—*New England Fish Chowder*

Kennedy, Mrs. Robert: widow of Attorney-General of the United States and U. S. Senator from New York—*Chocolate Roll*

King, Billie Jean: American tennis player, 19 Wimbledon titles; San Mateo, California—*Rice Casserole with Cheese*

Kirk, Mrs. Claude R., Jr.: wife of former Governor of Florida; Palm Beach—*Chicken Continental*

Landers, Ann (Mrs. Jules Lederer): author, columnist for Field Newspaper Syndicate; many awards; Chicago—*Noodle and Spinach Ring*

Landrieu, The Honorable Moon: American attorney; Mayor of New Orleans, Louisiana—*Stuffed Artichokes*

Lawrence, Carol (Mrs. Robert Goulet), *see* Goulet

Leeuwenberg, Mme Mimi: handwriting expert; Brussels, Belgium—*Yogurt Dessert*

Lehman, Mrs. Herbert: widow of former U. S. Senator from New York and Governor of New York; New York City—*Chocolate Mousse*

Lenya, Lotte: Austrian actress and singer; widow of Kurt Weill; Vienna, New York City—*Viennese Vacherin*

Lewis, Mr. and Mrs. Jerry: American film comedian and his wife; Hollywood—*Chicken Fricassee with Dumplings*

Lindstrom, Pia: television journalist, interviewer, WCBS-TV; New York City—*Mushroom and Onion Quiche*

Linkletter, Art: American television personality; "Mr. House Party"; Hollywood—*Strawberry Cheese Pie*

Lipman, Esther: Councilor; Adelaide, South Africa—*Seafood Ile de France*

Lowery, The Honorable Robert O.: first black Fire Commissioner of New York City—*Oxtail à la Catalane*

McCollum, Eleanor Searle Whitney: Locust Valley, New York, and Houston, Texas—*Frozen Orange Marshmallow Ice*

MacLaine, Shirley: American film actress, writer, director; author; Hollywood, New York City—*Stuffed Green Peppers*

Major, Mrs. Gerri: Senior Staff Editor, *Ebony*; New York City—*Choucroute Garnie*

Manilow, Barry: actor, rock superstar, recording artist; New York City—*Spaghetti with White Clam Sauce*

Martin, Mary: American stage actress and musical comedy star—*Aspic*

Mathis, Johnny: American singer and recording artist; master of "Mathis Magic"; Beverly Hills—*Wild Duck à la Mathis*

Meade, Julia: American film actress; New York City—*Roast Turkey with Corn Bread Stuffing*

Meany, George: American trade unionist; President, American Federation of Labor and Congress of Industrial Organizations; Washington, D. C.—*Vegetable-Beef Soup*

Meir, Golda: Israeli politician; former Prime Minister of Israel (1969-1974)—*Chicken Confetti*

Mejia, Tomás Heli Cardona: Universidad Libre de Colombia, Bogotá—*Roast Leg of Lamb with Flageolets*

Merrill, Dina: American leading lady on stage and screen; New York City—*Fruit Cup with Wine*

Merrill, Robert: American baritone; many opera, concert and television appearances in United States and Europe; New York City—*Chicken Livers Chasseur*

Mesta, Perle (1893-1975): former U. S. Minister to Luxembourg; Washington society hostess—*Seafood Newburg in Crêpes*

Miller, Mrs. Leonard: international socialite; Sussex, England—*Peas Braised with Lettuce and Onions*

Minnelli, Liza: American actress and singer, stage and screen—*Chiles Rellenos*

Mitchell, Jack: photographer; internationally known for theater photographs; New York City—*Cold Yogurt Soup*

Mondale, Mr. and Mrs. Walter F. (Joan Mondale): Vice-President of the United States, and his wife—*Pumpkin Bread*

Monroe, Marilyn (1926-1962): American film

legend—*Vegetable Cocktail*

Moreno, Mario (Cantinflas), *see* Cantinflas

Morgan, Rose: President, House of Beauty, New York City—*Honey Buns*

Mountbatten, Louis, Earl Mountbatten of Burma: Admiral of the Fleet, former Governor-General of India; Romsey, London, England; Sligo, Ireland—*Leg of Venison with Peach Sauce*

Nearing, Vivienne W.: attorney, partner in Stroock & Stroock & Lavan; New York City—*Chicken with Orange*

Neiman, LeRoy: American artist; many international exhibitions, many prizes; New York City—*Midnight Chops for Two*

Newman, Isidore, II: American retired business executive; active in community service; New Orleans—*Choucroute*

Nixon, Agnes: packager and chief writer for "One Life to Live" and "All My Children," WABC-TV; New York City—*Mushroom Soufflé*

Nixon, Richard Milhous: President of the United States (1969-1974)—*Cheesecake*

Nixon, Mrs. Richard Milhous (Pat Nixon): former First Lady of the United States—*Country Omelet*

Palmer, Mr. and Mrs. Arnold (Winnie Palmer): American professional golfer and business executive; winner of 79 professional titles; Youngstown, Pennsylvania—*Hawaiian Meatballs with Sweet-Sour Sauce*

Paterson, The Honorable Basil A.: Secretary of State, The State of New York; American attorney; Democratic National Committeeman from New York—*Black Bean Soup*

Poston, The Honorable Mrs. Ersa H.: President, New York State Civil Service Commission; many awards; Albany—*Poston's Pre-Payday Casserole*

Premice, Josephine: international chanteuse; Paris, New York City—*Sweet Potato Soufflé*

Preminger, The Honorable Dr. Marion Mill (1913-1972): former Consul General to Gabon—*Lamb and Chicken Gabonais with Green Rice Ring*

Quintero, José: Panamanian-born stage director; many awards; New York City—*Spaghetti with Panamanian Cold Shrimp Sauce*

Rabin, Mrs. Yitzhak (Leah Schlossberg): wife of former Prime Minister of Israel—*Stuffed Green Peppers in Tomato Sauce*

Rampal, Jean-Pierre Louis: French flautist, conductor, teacher; many awards; Paris—*Eggs Mamette*

Randolph, A. Philip: American labor leader; Vice-President AFL-CIO; New York City—*Baked Beans*

Rangel, The Honorable Charles B.: American attorney; U. S. Representative from New York; New York City—*Chicken Pilau*

Raye, Martha (Margie Yvonne Reed): American actress, vaudeville, stage, films; Hollywood—*Garden Bouillon*

Reagan, Mrs. Ronald (Nancy Reagan): former First Lady of California; Sacramento—*Elegant Flaming Beef*

Redford, Robert: actor, television, films; Lola is Mrs. Redford—*Lola's Whole-Wheat Quick Bread*

Reed, Rex: journalist; motion picture critic; New York City—*Shrimp Gumbo*

Reed, Willis: coach of New York Knickerbockers; former basketball player, Podoloff Cup (most valuable player), 1969-1970; New York City—*Casserole of Calico Bass, Shrimps and Crab*

Reynolds, Debbie: American comedienne and musical star; Beverly Hills—*Hush Puppies*

Richman, Harry (1855-1972): American entertainer; "Mr. Birth of the Blues"—*Fruta Almina*

Roberts, Dr. and Mrs. Oral (Evelyn Roberts): Founder and President, Oral Roberts Evangelistic Association, Inc.; President, Oral Roberts University; Tulsa, Oklahoma—*Red Devil's-Food Cake*

Robinson, Bill "Bojangles" (1878-1949): American entertainer and tap-dancer—*Cocktail Meatballs*

Rockefeller, Nelson A.: former Governor of New York State; former Vice-President of the United States—*New York State Flat Apple Pie*

Rockefeller, Mrs. Nelson A. (Margaretta Fitler Rockefeller): former first lady of New York State—*Duckling with Black Cherry Sauce*

Roosevelt, Mrs. Eleanor (1884-1962): former First Lady of the United States; U. S. Representative to United Nations General Assembly, 1945-1953—*Nesselrode Pie with Infallible Piecrust*

Rubenstein, Madame Helena (Princess Gourielli) (1871-1965): international cosmetician—*Coconut Fudge Cake*

el-Sadat, Anwar: President of the United Arab Republic, Egypt; Cairo—*Baked Fish*

Samuels, Howard: American businessman, politician, author, lecturer; New York City—*Spanakopita (Greek Spinach Pies)*

Schwarzenegger, Arnold: Mr. Olympia; Austrian bodybuilder—*Roast Marinated Beef*

Sharp, Saundra: American actress and singer; New York City—*French-Fried Cauliflower with Minted Peas*

Sihanouk, Princess Monique: wife of the former King of Cambodia—*Sautéed Doves*

Sills, Beverly: American soprano; opera performances in United States, Europe, Latin America; numerous recitals; New York City—*Sukiyaki*

Simons, Syd: makeup artist and hair stylist; Chicago—*Syd's Oriental Steak*

Sims, Naomi: founder of Naomi Sims Collection (wigs); former model, Model of the Year, 1967, 1970; New York City—*Steak and Kidney Pie*

Slate, Richard: public relations specialist; Brooklyn, New York—*Poulet d'Amour*

Sleeper, Martha: international hostess; former film actress; Old San Juan, Puerto Rico—*Mushroom and Spinach Salad*

Smith, Liz: American syndicated columnist; New York City—*Texas Chicken-Fried Steak*

Snyder, Tom: American television news personality; host of "Tomorrow," WNBC-TV; Los Angeles—*Heavenly Hamburger*

Spitz, Mrs. Leo: Palm Springs, Beverly Hills, Paris—*Ratatouille*

Stokes, Carl: American attorney and politician; news commentator, WNBC-TV; New York City—*Savory Roast Beef*

Sullivan, Ed (1902-1974): newspaper columnist; television personality ("Ed Sullivan Show," 1948-1971)—*My Mother's Bread Pudding*

Summer, Donna: American rock star and recording artist; Los Angeles—*Summer Schnitzel*

Susskind, Mrs. David: wife of the television producer; New York City—*Chicken in a Pot*

Sutton, The Honorable Percy E.: attorney, political leader, former president of the Borough of Manhattan; New York City—*Baked Red Snapper with Party Sauce*

Taylor, Elizabeth (Mrs. John William Warner): actress; humanitarian; child film star; M.G.M. star; Academy Awards: 1960 for *Butterfield 8*; 1966 for *Who's Afraid of Virginia Woolf*—*Quiche Lorraine*

Trigère, Pauline: Parisian-born dress designer; many awards; New York City—*Rice Pauline*

Trudeau, The Honorable Pierre Elliot: Canadian lawyer and politician; Prime Minister of Canada; Ottawa—*Batter-Fried Vegetables*

Tubman, Mrs. William V. S.: widow of the President of Liberia; Monrovia—*Chicken and Groundnut Stew*

Tucker, Sophie (1884-1966): Russian-born American singer and entertainer, in vaudeville, musical comedy, films; international acclaim; "The Last of the Red Hot Mammas"—*Gefilte Fish*

Ullman, Liv: Norwegian actress, stage and films; many awards; Los Angeles—*Norjapcan Foo Young and Vegetables*

Vanburen, Abigail (Pauline Friedman Phillips): writer, lecturer, syndicated columnist; many awards; Beverly Hills—*Abby's Pecan Pie*

Vance, The Honorable Cyrus: United States Secretary of State; Washington, D. C.—*Shrimps au Gratin*

Wagner, Susan (Mrs. Robert F. Wagner) (1910-1964): former First Lady of New York City—*Cheese Straws*

Waldheim, Mrs. Kurt (Elisabeth Ritschel): wife of Secretary-General of the United Nations; Vienna, New York City—*Soufflé Rothschild*

Walters, Barbara: American newswoman and television broadcaster; author—*My Mother's Stuffed Cabbage Rolls*

Washington, Mrs. Bennetta (Mrs. Walter E. Washington): wife of the Commissioner of District of Columbia and Mayor of Washington, D. C.—*Edna's Beef Cacciatora*

Weill, Lotte Lenya, *see* Lenya

Williams, Mrs. Jaymie B.: international socialite; Miami—*Spinach Soufflé*

Wilson, Mr. and Mrs. Earl: syndicated columnist, *The New York Post*; radio commentator, editor; New York City—*Roast Turkey Gourmet*

Wilson, Erica: Queen of the Needle Works; columnist, *New York Daily News;* New York City—*Toad in a Hole*

Wilson, John Louis, A.I.A.: first black architect to be licensed in New York State—*Louisiana Jambalaya*

Wright, Jane Cooke, M. D.: physician, college dean, specialist in chemotherapy; many awards; New York City—*Party Roast Beef with Onion Pie*

Young, The Honorable Andrew: U. S. Ambassador to the United Nations; clergyman, former Congressman; New Orleans, New York City—*Seafood from the Bayou*

In addition to the contributors listed, many other good friends sent recipes or ideas for favorite dishes. Their contributions have been omitted only because there wasn't enough room. Thanks to all of them for their support of the Educational Guild.

# Index of Recipes

---

208

210